William Enfield

Sermons on Practical Subjects

Second Edition, Vol. 1

William Enfield

Sermons on Practical Subjects
Second Edition, Vol. 1

ISBN/EAN: 9783337160609

Printed in Europe, USA, Canada, Australia, Japan

Cover: Foto ©Lupo / pixelio.de

More available books at **www.hansebooks.com**

SERMONS

ON

PRACTICAL SUBJECTS,

BY THE LATE
W. ENFIELD, LL.D.

PREPARED FOR THE PRESS BY HIMSELF.

To which are prefixed
MEMOIRS OF THE AUTHOR,
BY J. AIKIN, M.D.

IN THREE VOLUMES.

SECOND EDITION.

VOL. I.

LONDON:
PRINTED FOR J. JOHNSON, IN ST. PAUL'S CHURCH-YARD.

1799.

BIOGRAPHICAL ACCOUNT

OF THE

AUTHOR OF THESE VOLUMES.

The Rev. William Enfield, LL.D. was born at Sudbury in Suffolk, on March 29, 1741, O.S. In common with many other characters of moral and literary excellence, it was his lot to come into the world destitute of the advantages of birth or fortune. His parents were in a humble condition of life, which they rendered respectable by their virtues. His early education was probably on the narrow scale marked out by his circumstances. By his amiable disposition and promising parts

parts he recommended himself to the Rev. Mr. Hextall, the dissenting minister of the place, who treated him with peculiar notice, and took pleasure in forming his youthful mind. He particularly awakened in him a sensibility to the beauties of our principal poets; among whom, Akenside, by the charms of his versification, and the exalted tone of his philosophy, was a peculiar favourite both with the instructor and the pupil. It appears to me no unreasonable supposition that to his early fondness for this author, Dr. Enfield was indebted, more than to any other single circumstance, for that uniform purity of language, that entire freedom from any thing like vulgarity, as well in conversation as in writing, by which he was ever distinguished. Mr. Hextall's good opinion was probably the chief cause of his being devoted to the christian ministry. In his 17th year he was sent to the academy at Daventry, then conducted by the Rev. Dr. Ashworth.

worth. At this seminary he passed through the usual course of preparatory study for the pulpit. Of his academical character I know no more than that he was always conspicuous for the elegance of his compositions; and that he was among the number of those students whose inquiries led them to adopt a less rigid system of christianity than was the established doctrine of the place.

It was a striking proof of the attractions he possessed as a preacher, and as an amiable man in society, that almost immediately on leaving the academy he was invited to undertake the office of sole minister to the congregation of Benn's Garden in Liverpool, one of the most respectable among the dissenters. To that situation he was ordained in November 1763; and in a town abounding with agreeable society, and distinguished by liberal sentiments and hospitable manners, he passed seven of the happiest years of his life. He married, in 1767, Mary, the only daughter of Mr. Holland, draper in Liverpool; and a moſt cordial union of thirty years gave full proof of the felicity of his choice. Though greatly engaged both in the pleaſant intercourſes of ſociety, and in the ſerious duties of his office, he commenced in this place his literary career with two volumes of ſermons, printed in 1768 and 1770, which were very favourably received by the public. Their pleaſing moral ſtrain, marked by no ſyſtematic peculiarities, ſo well adapted them for general uſe, that many congregations, beſides that in which they were originally preached, had the benefit of the inſtruction they conveyed. A collection of Hymns, for the uſe of his congregation, and of Family Prayers of his own compoſition, for private uſe, further added to his profeſſional and literary reputation.

On the death of the Rev. Mr. Seddon of Warrington, Mr. Enfield was one of the firſt perſons thought of by the truſtees of

the

the academical inſtitution founded in that place, to ſucceed him in the offices of tutor in the belles-lettres, and of reſident conductor of the diſcipline, under the title of *Rector Academiæ*. With reſpect to his fitneſs for the firſt no doubt could be entertained. The ſecond was an untried exertion, depending for its ſucceſs upon qualities of temper rarely meeting in one individual. Whatever could be effected by thoſe amiable endowments which conciliate affection, might be hoped from one who was become the delight of a large circle of acquaintance; but in thoſe emergencies where firmneſs, reſolution, and a kind of dignified ſeverity of conduct might be requiſite, there was cauſe to apprehend a failure. He had his miſgivings, but they were overcome by the encouragement and importunity of friends; and the offered ſituation was in ſeveral reſpects ſuch as might flatter a young man, fond of literary ſociety, and ambitious of a proper field for the diſplay of his talents. He accepted it, together with the office of minister to the dissenting congregation of Warrington. The occupations in which he engaged were extensive and complicated; but no man had ever a better right to confide in his own industry and readiness.

Every one acquainted with the attempts that have been made by the dissenters to institute places of education for the advanced periods of youth, must have been sensible of the extreme difficulty of uniting the liberal plan of a collegiate life with such a system of internal discipline as shall secure sobriety of manners, and diligence in the pursuit of study. Those sanctions which, however imperfectly, serve as engines of government in seminaries established by the state, must ever be wanting in private institutions, which cannot annex to the grossest violation of their laws a higher penalty than simple expulsion, followed by no disabilities or deprivations, and probably held extremely cheap

cheap by thofe who have moft deferved it. Warrington had a full fhare of this difficulty; and alfo laboured under others, which rendered its exiftence, though at times it appeared flourifhing and refpectable, little better than a long ftruggle againft incurable difeafe. The efforts of Dr. Enfield were faithfully joined, with thofe of his colleagues, to fupport its credit, and to remedy evils as they occurred. His diligence was exemplary; his fervices as a public and private tutor were numerous and valuable; his attention to difcipline was, at leaft, uninterrupted; but it may be acknowledged that the arduous poft of domeftic fuperintendant, and enforcer of the laws, was not that for which he was beft calculated. So fenfible, indeed, was he of his deficiency in this refpect, and fo much did he find his tranquillity injured by the fcenes to which he was expofed, that he made a very ferious attempt to free himfelf from the burden, by refigning this

part

part of his charge; and it was only after the failure of various applications by the truſtees to engage a ſucceſſor, that he ſuffered himſelf to be perſuaded to retain it. In fine, the criſis of the inſtitution arrived in 1783, and its embarraſſments were cured by its diſſolution.

However toilſome and anxious this period of Dr. Enfield's life might have been, it was that of rapid mental improvement. By the company he kept, and the buſineſs he had to go through, his faculties were ſtrained to full exertion: nor was it only as a tutor that he employed his talents; he greatly extended his reputation as a writer. The following liſt compriſes thoſe works which he publiſhed during his reſidence at Warrington. Several of them belong to the humble but uſeful claſs of compilations; yet in them he found occaſion to diſplay the elegance of his taſte, and the ſoundneſs of his judgment.

A Sermon at the Ordination of the Rev. Philip Taylor; 1770.

The Preacher's Directory; 1771, 4to.

The English Preacher; a collection of Sermons abridged and selected from various Authors; 9 vols. 12mo. 1773.

An Essay toward the History of Liverpool, from the Papers of the late Mr. George Perry, with other materials since collected; small fol. 1774.

Observations on Literary Property; 4to. 1774.

The Speaker; or Miscellaneous Pieces selected from the best English Writers, for the purposes of Reading and Speaking; 8vo. 1774. To this very popular Work was prefixed an Essay on Elocution; and to a subsequent edition was subjoined an Essay on Reading Works of Taste.

Biographical Sermons, on the principal characters mentioned in the Old and New Testament; 12mo. 1777.

A Sermon on the Death of Mr. J. Gallway, a Student in the Academy at Warrington; 1777.

A Sermon on the Ordination of the Rev. J. Prior Estlin; 1778.

A Sermon on the Death of the Rev. J. Aikin, D.D. 1780.

Exercises in Elocution, being a sequel to the Speaker;

Speaker; 8vo. 1781. To an edition of this in 1794 was added, Counsels for Young Men.

A Collection of Hymns; intended as a supplement to Watts's Psalms; 1781.

A Translation of Rossignol's Elements of Geometry; 8vo.

Institutes of Natural Philosophy, Theoretical and Experimental; 4to. 1783.

It will be remarked, that mathematical science is included among the latter topics; and no circumstance is better adapted to give an idea of the power of his mind than the occasion and manner of his taking up this abstruse study, which had previously by no means been a favourite with him. On a vacancy in the mathematical department of the academy it was found impracticable to give adequate encouragement from the funds it possessed to a separate tutor in that branch. Dr. Enfield was therefore strongly urged to undertake it; and by the hard study of one vacation he qualified himself to set out with a new class, which he instructed ed with great clearnefs and precifion; himfelf advancing in the fcience in proportion to the demand, till he became a very excellent teacher in all the parts which were requifite in the academical courfe.

The degree of doctor of laws, which added a new title to his name during his refidence at Warrington, was conferred upon him by the univerfity of Edinburgh.

After the diffolution of the academy, Dr. Enfield remained two years at Warrington, occupied in the education of private pupils, a fmall number of whom he took as boarders, and in the care of his congregation. For the inftruction of the latter he drew up a feries of difcourfes on the principal incidents and moral precepts of the gofpel, in which he difplayed both his talents as a commentator, and his fkill in expanding into general leffons of conduct, thofe hints and particular obfervations which occur in the facred sacred narratives. This will not be an improper place to give some account of Dr. Enfield's character as a preacher and a divine. His manner of delivery was grave and impressive, affecting rather a tenor of uniform dignity than a variety of expression, for which his voice was not well calculated. It was entirely free from what is called *tone*, and though not highly animated, was by no means dull, and never careless or indifferent. As to his matter, it was almost exclusively that of a *moral preacher*. Religion was to him rather a principle than a sentiment; and he was more solicitous to deduce from it *a rule of life*, enforced by its peculiar sanctions, than to elevate it into a source of sublime feeling. Despising superstition, and fearing enthusiasm, he held as of inferior value every thing in religion which could not ally itself with morality, and condescend to human uses. His theological system was purged of every mysterious or unintelligible proposition; it

included

included nothing which appeared to him irreconcileable with found philofophy, and the moſt rational opinions concerning the divine nature and perfections. Poſſibly the teſt of rationality might with him fuperfede that of literary criticifm. It will be feen from the fubjects felected for this publication, that moral topics were much more congenial to him than doctrinal ones; and his character as a public inſtructor muſt be derived from the manner in which he has treated thefe. Probably it will be found that fcarcely any writer has entered with more delicacy into the minute and lefs obvious points of morality—has more ſkilfully marked out the nice difcriminations of virtue and vice, of the fit and unfit. He has not only delineated the path of the ſtrictly right, but of the amiable and becoming. He has aimed at rendering mankind not only mutually ferviceable, but mutually agreeable; and has delighted in painting true goodnefs with all thofe

colours

colours which it was said of old would make her so enchanting should she ever become visible to mortal eyes.

It will, perhaps, be expected that something should be said of Dr. Enfield in the peculiar character of a *Dissenter*. To *dissent* was by no means a part of his natural disposition; on the contrary, he could not without a struggle differ from those whom he saw dignified by station, respectable for learning and morals, and amiable in the intercourse of society. Nor was the voice of authority, when mildly and reasonably exerted, a signal to him of resistance, but rather a call to acquiescence. It is therefore not to be wondered at, that there was a period in his life when he looked towards the religious establishment of his country with a wish that no insuperable barrier should exist to the exclusion of those who, without violating the absolute dictates of conscience, might desire to join it. Inclined by temper and system to think well of mankind, and

and to entertain fanguine hopes of their progrefs towards truth and reafon, he could not bring himfelf to imagine that the active efforts (which we may all remember) of many excellent perfons to produce a further reform in the Englifh church, and render the terms of entrance into its miniftry more eafy and liberal, would in the end fail of their effect. This idea dwelt long and weightily on his mind, and difpofed him rather to regard the conformities, than the differences, between fyftems which he expected to fee continually more nearly approaching each other. Moreover, the correct and elegant language, and the manly ftrain of morality, which then characterifed the pulpit compofitions of the moft eminent of the clergy, commanded his entire approbation; and he thought that a mutual oblivion of topics of controverfy might take place, from a confent in all friends of rational religion to confine their public difcourfes to fub-

jects on which no differences existed between them. He lived, however, to see all his expectations of this amicable union frustrated — to see hierarchical claims maintained more dogmatically than before—and the chief stress of religion placed upon those doctrines in which the English church-articles most differ from the opinions of that class of dissenters to which he belonged. He lived, therefore, to become a more decided separatist than ever; and I am sure, that for many years before his death, though all his personal candour and good-will towards the opposite party remained, no consideration would have induced him to range himself under its banners. The rights of private judgment and public discussion, and all the fundamental points of civil and religious liberty, were become more and more dear to him; and he asserted them with a courage and zeal which seemed scarcely to have belonged to his habitual temper. A very manly discourse, which
he

he published in 1788, on the hundredth anniverfary of the revolution, fufficiently teftifies his fentiments on thefe important fubjects.

It is now time to return to biographical narrative. In 1785, receiving an invitation from the octagon-diffenting congregation at Norwich, a fociety with whom any man might efteem it an honour and happinefs to be connected, he accepted it, under the condition of refiding at a fmall diftance from the city, and continuing his plan of domeftic education. He firft settled at the pleafant village of Thorpe; but at length he found it more convenient to remove to Norwich itfelf. Though he was eminently happy in his mode of educating a fmall number, of which feveral ftriking examples might be adduced, yet, like moft who have adopted that plan, he found that the difficulty of keeping up a regular fupply of pupils, and the unpleafant reftraint arifing from a party of young men,

men, so far domiciliated, that they left neither time nor place for family privacy, more than compensated the advantages to be derived from such an employment of his talents. He finally removed, therefore, to a smaller habitation, entirely declined receiving boarders, and only gave private instructions to two or three select pupils a few hours in the forenoon. At length he determined to be perfectly master of his own time, and to give to his family, friends, and spontaneous literary pursuits, all the leisure he possessed from his professional duties. The circumstances of his family confirmed him in this resolution. He was the father of two sons and three daughters, all educated under his own eye; and had he had no other examples to produce of his power of making himself at the same time a friend and a tutor—of conciliating the most tender affection with ready and undeviating obedience—his children would, by all who knew them,

be

be admitted as sufficient proofs of this happy art. They became every thing that their parents could wish;—but the eldest son, after passing with uncommon reputation through his clerkship to an attorney (Mr. Roscoe, of Liverpool), and advancing so far in his professional career as to be appointed, when just of age, town-clerk of Nottingham, was suddenly snatched away by a fever. The doctor bore his grievous loss with exemplary resignation; but the struggle produced effects on his health which alarmed his friends. Symptoms resembling those of the fatal disease termed *Angina Pectoris* came on; indeed, it may be said, that he really laboured under an incipient state of this disorder. But time, medicine, and happier subjects of reflection, restored him to health and cheerfulness. He had the felicity of seeing two of his daughters most desirably settled in marriage. His remaining son bid fair to become all that the other had been. He was,

was, therefore, fully entitled to enjoy himself in the domeſtic freedom he loved, and to confine his future exertions to thoſe lettered employments which, to one of his induſtrious habits, were neceſſary to give a zeſt to ſocial relaxation.

He had not yet completely detached himſelf from the buſineſs of tuition, when he undertook the moſt laborious of his literary taſks, an abridgment of " Brucker's Hiſtory of Philoſophy." This work appeared in two volumes 4to. in the year 1791, and would alone have been ſufficient to eſtabliſh the writer's character as a maſter of the middle ſtyle of compoſition, and as a judicious ſelector of what was moſt valuable in the repreſentation of manners and opinions. The original work has obtained a high reputation among the learned, for the depth of its reſearches, and the liberality of its ſpirit; but its Latin ſtyle is involved and prolix, and the heavineſs that pervades the whole has rendered it rather a book for occaſional

fional confultation than for direct perufal.
Dr. Enfield's abridgment is a work equally
inftructive and agreeable; and it may be
pronounced that the tenets of all the leading fects of philofophers were never before, in the Englifh language, difplayed
with fuch elegance and perfpicuity. It
was, indeed, his peculiar talent to arrange
and exprefs other men's ideas to the greateft
advantage. His ftyle, chafte, clear, correct,
free from all affectation and fingularity,
was proper for all topics; and the fpirit
of method and order which reigned in
his own mind, communicated itfelf to
every fubject which he touched upon.
Thefe qualities, together with that candour which was interwoven in his very
conftitution, efpecially fitted him to take
a part in a literary journal; and to one of
the moft refpectable of thefe works he
was long a confiderable contributor. The
inftitution of a new magazine, under the
name of the *Monthly*, which in its plan
embraced a larger circle of original lite-
rature

rature than ufual with thefe mifcellanies, engaged him to exercife his powers as an effayift on a variety of topics; and the papers with which he enriched it, under the title of the *Inquirer*, obtained great applaufe from the manly freedom of their fentiment, and the correct elegance of their language.

Thus did his latter years glide on, tranquil and ferene, in the bofom of domeftic comfort, furrounded by friends to whom he became continually more dear, and in the midft of agreeable occupations. So well confirmed did his health appear, and fo much did he feel himfelf in the full vigour and maturity of his powers, that he did not hefitate, in the year 1796, to affociate himfelf with the writer of this account, one of his oldeft and moft intimate companions, in a literary undertaking of great magnitude, which looked to a diftant period for its completion. Were it not the duty of mortals to employ their talents in the way they

they can approve, without regarding contingencies which they can neither foresee nor overrule, such an engagement, in persons descending into the vale of years, might be accused of presumption: but it implied in them no more than a resolution to act with diligence as long as they should be permitted to act—to work while it is called to-day, mindful of that approaching night when no man can work. The composition, that of a *General Biographical Dictionary*, proved so agreeable to Dr. Enfield, that he was often heard to say his hours of study had never passed so pleasantly with him; and the progress he made was proportioned to his industry and good-will. Every circumstance seemed to promise him years of comfort in store. He was happy himself, and imparted that happiness to all who came within the sphere of his influence. But an incurable disease was in the mean time making unsuspected advances. A scirrhous contraction of the rectum, denoting

noting itself only by symptoms which he did not understand, and which, therefore, he imperfectly described to his medical friends, was preparing, without pain or general disease, to effect a sudden and irresistible change. The very day before this disorder manifested itself he was complimented on his cheerful spirits, and healthy looks, and himself confessed that he had nothing, bodily or mental, of which he ought to complain. But the obstruction was now formed. A sickness came on, the proper functions of the intestines were suspended, nothing was able to give relief, and after a week, passed rather in constant uneasiness than in acute pain, with his faculties entire nearly to the last, foreseeing the fatal event, and meeting it with manly fortitude, he sunk in the arms of his children and friends, and expired without a struggle. This catastrophe took place on Nov. 3, 1797, in the fifty-seventh year of his life. The deep regrets of all who knew

knew him—of those the most to whom he was best known—render it unnecessary to enter into any further description of a character, the essence of which was *to be amiable*. A man's writings have often proved very inadequate tests of his dispositions. Those of Dr. Enfield, however, are not. They breathe the very spirit of his gentle and generous soul. He loved mankind, and wished nothing so much as to render them the worthy objects of love. This is the leading character of the discourses here selected for publication; as it is, indeed, of all he composed. May their effect equal the most sanguine wishes of their benevolent author!

J. AIKIN.

London, April 10, 1798.

1

CONTENTS.

On the Omnipresence of God.

PSALM cxxxix. 7.

Whither shall I go from thy Spirit? or whither shall I flee from thy presence?

p. 1

On the Faithfulness of God.

DEUTERONOMY vii. 9.

Know therefore that the Lord thy God, he is God, the FAITHFUL *God.* - 21

Characters of the Works of God.

REVELATION xv. 3.

Great and marvellous are thy works, Lord God Almighty! - - - 41

The Christian Religion, a valuable Treasure.

MATTHEW xiii. 44.

The kingdom of heaven is like unto treasure hid in a field; which, when a man hath found, he hideth, and for joy thereof, goeth and selleth all that he hath and buyeth that field - p. 63

On the moral Abuse of Words.

ISAIAH v. 20.

Woe unto them that call evil good, and good evil - - - - - 86

Against thinking ill of the World.

PSALM cxvi. 11.

I said in my haste, All men are liars 109

Inattention to the Concerns of others reproved.

GENESIS iv. 9.

Am I my brother's keeper? - 12

Chara*c*ters

Characters of Charity.

1 COR. xiii. 4, 5.

Charity suffereth long, and is kind; charity envieth not; charity vaunteth not itself, is not puffed up; doth not behave itself unseemly; seeketh not her own; is not easily provoked; thinketh no evil. p. 151

Characters of Charity.

1 COR. xiii. 6—8.

Charity rejoiceth not in iniquity, but rejoiceth in the truth; beareth all things; believeth all things; hopeth all things; endureth all things: charity never faileth.

174

The good Man secure from Shame.

PSALM cxix. 6.

Then I shall not be ashamed, when I have respect unto all thy commandments 198

Against

Against Evil-speaking.

TITUS iii. 2.

Put them in mind—to speak evil of no man - - - - p. 217

On Industry.

ROM. xii. 11.

Not slothful in business - 239

Caution in forming, and Constancy in preserving, Friendships recommended.

PROVERBS xxvii. 10.

Thine own friend, and thy father's friend, forsake not - - - 261

Prayer for a Competency.

PROVERBS xxx. 8.

Feed me with food convenient for me 280

Youth

Youth and Age compared.

PSALM xxxvii. 25.

I have been young, and now am old p. 300

On Humility.

ROMANS xii. 3.

I say, through the grace given unto me, to every man that is among you, not to think of himself more highly than he ought to think - - - - 327

The Value of Moral Wisdom.

PROVERBS iv. 17.

Wisdom is the principal thing; therefore get wisdom - - - 349

On the Necessity of establishing good Principles, and fixing a prudent Plan of Conduct, in early Life.

PROVERBS iv. 26.

Ponder the path of thy feet, that all thy ways may be established - 372

The

The Nature, Caufes, and Folly, of Self-deception.

PROVERBS xvi. 3.

All the ways of a man are clean in his own eyes, but the Lord weigheth the fpirits

P. 395

Contentment and Generofity exemplified in the Conduct of Efau.

GENESIS xxxiii. 9.

And Efau faid, I have enough, my brother; keep that thou haft unto thyfelf - 417

SERMONS,

SERMONS, &c.

On the Omnipresence of God.

PSALM cxxxix. 7.

Whither shall I go from thy Spirit? or whither shall I flee from thy presence?

WHEN ignorant mortals attempt to think and speak concerning the nature of the one infinite and eternal Deity, what can be expected but that their conceptions should be feeble, and their representations inadequate? If there be mysteries in the smallest particle of matter, which the most perfect human understanding cannot unfold, who can wonder that we cannot find out the Almighty to perfection?

Self-exiftence, infinity, and eternity, are ideas too vaft for the human intellect to comprehend: fuch knowledge is too wonderful for us; it is high, we cannot attain unto it. It furely requires no extraordinary fhare of modefty to acknowledge, that there may exift an Intelligent Being, whofe nature is underived, whofe duration is eternal, and whofe prefence is univerfal, although the manner in which fuch a Being exifts be to us wholly unknown.

That fuch a Being *doth* exift, and that he is endued with every poffible perfection, the frame and conftitution of nature fully demonftrate. The marks of active intelligence force themfelves upon our obfervation wherever we turn our eyes, and leave us no room to doubt that the univerfe is the work of an almighty and moft fkilful Architect, who founded the earth by his wifdom, and ftretched out the heavens by his underftanding. And the fame arguments which prove the exiftence istence of this great Being, likewise evince his universal presence. A few words may suffice to explain the grounds of this great article of our faith; for they are obvious to every understanding, and universally acknowledged to be conclusive. Our great business is to impress upon our minds such a conviction of this important truth as shall render it habitually influential upon our conduct.

We observe in nature an immense variety of operations continually carrying on, which are the manifest effects of power and wisdom, and which therefore necessarily suppose the presence of a wise and powerful Agent. If all nature be full of astonishing effects of skill and energy, all nature must be full of God. Motion is every where observed, throughout the material world, to follow certain settled laws, and to be so conducted as to answer the wisest ends. What can we infer from these appearances, but the continual agency of an intelligent and powerful Deity?

Deity? Since similar effects are every where produced from similar causes, there must be an intelligent Being every where present, who preserves the uniformity and harmony of nature. We cannot form a more philosophical idea of the laws of nature, than to consider them as the established manner in which the Deity executes the purposes of his wisdom.

And if a power be universally exerted to preserve the order of nature, it is evident that the Being in whom this power resides must be every where present. The Eternal mind, on whom all nature depends—who causes the revolutions of day and night, summer and winter—who supports the whole animal and intellectual world in that beautiful regularity which he at first established—who inspires all nature with life and joy—must fill the universe with his presence. All things remain as they were from the beginning, because all nature is animated by a wise, powerful, and good Being, who ordereth all

all things according to the counsel of his will.

Nor is there any thing in the supposition of the universal presence and perpetual agency of the Supreme Being inconsistent either with his dignity or his felicity. Men who measure great things by small, may be ready to imagine it beneath the majesty of the Lord of All, to concern himself in the minute affairs of the creation, or to suppose that it would be an interruption of his felicity to be perpetually employed in conducting the operations of nature. But it is absurd to suppose that an all-powerful Being can be wearied by labour, or that it is unworthy of the excellent nature of Deity to be ever active in supporting and blessing the creatures which his goodness inclined him to form.

The universal presence of an Intelligent mind, necessarily includes the idea of universal knowledge. That great Being, who fills every portion of space, must at the same time be intimately acquainted with every thing that exifts. The univerfe, in all its parts, is continually under the Divine infpection, and he comprehends in one view the immenfity of the creation. Boundlefs as the Divine works are—and philofophy difcovers to us worlds beyond worlds in endlefs progreffion—they all lie open to the view of the Supreme Being: being ever prefent in all worlds, he furveys the whole, and every part, with a degree of exactnefs which nothing can efcape. His intelligent creatures, which are innumerable, are all perfectly known to the Divine mind.

Thefe fentiments are no where expreffed in fuch fublime and animated language, as in the Pfalm from which the text is taken—" Whither fhall I go from thy Spirit? or whither fhall I flee from thy prefence? If I afcend up into heaven, thou art there; if I make my bed in the grave, behold, thou art there: if I take the wings of the morning, and dwell in the uttermoft parts of the fea; even there fhall shall thy hand lead me, and thy right hand shall hold me: if I say, Surely the darkness shall cover me; even the night shall be light about me."

Such are the conceptions which the most accurate reasoning, as well as the language of the holy Scriptures, teach us to entertain concerning the Supreme Being: and it is of great moment that they should be firmly established in our minds, and frequently recollected, both to correct and exalt our notions of God and religion, and to furnish us with powerful principles of right conduct, and an inexhaustible source of consolation.

It is not, perhaps, an easy thing entirely to divest our minds of all gross and vulgar ideas of God, or to purify our devotions from all mixture of superstition: but nothing will so effectually enable us to do this, as a due attention to that attribute of the divine nature which is the subject of our present meditations. If God be every where present, it is very evident, that he cannot be more in one place than in another; and, confequently, that there is no one part of the univerfe which ought to be confidered as the refidence or habitation of the Almighty more than the reft. There may be particular regions of his immenfe empire in which he may choofe to make diftinguifhed difplays of his power and greatnefs: there may be focieties of rational beings, inhabiting fome of thofe innumerable worlds which occupy univerfal fpace, whom he honours with peculiar manifeftations of his goodnefs: fuch a region is, according to the promifes of the gofpel of Chrift, provided for good men after death, under the name of *heaven*. But we ought not to imagine the Great Firft Being, who is the caufe and fupport of all being, life, order, and happinefs, throughout the vaft univerfe, refiding in a palace, feated upon a throne, and dwelling in the midft of a fphere of light, too dazzling for mortal eyes, where he is furrounded with a numerous train

of

of bright and glorious attendants, which are continually proſtrating themſelves at his footſtool. Such deſcriptions of Deity as theſe are evidently borrowed from human affairs; and wherever they are introduced, are only to be conſidered as figurative illuſtrations of a ſubject which is too exalted for human comprehenſion. If they be underſtood merely in this light, they may, like all other metaphorical expreſſions of abſtract truths or ſpiritual objects, be of uſe to give us a lively impreſſion and a ſtrong feeling of the ſubject: but the utmoſt care ſhould be taken not to miſtake metaphorical language for literal truth, leſt thoſe ſublime images, which are intended to aſſiſt devotion, ſhould in fact encourage ſuperſtition, and lead us to think the Great Univerſal Mind "altogether ſuch an one as ourſelves." It may, perhaps, ſeem unneceſſary to add, that we ſhould be careful that we be not led by the figurative application of terms expreſſing any parts of the human body, as eyes, ears,

ears, and hands, to the Deity, into any gross conceptions of this Great Being under a human form: and yet there can be little doubt, that children and others, whose imaginations are stronger than their judgments, are in some danger of such misapprehensions; and the rather, as there have been, and still are, opinions professed among some sects of Christians which favour these vulgar errors. There have been Christian societies, whose distinguishing tenet has been, that God subsists truly and literally in a human form: and the number of Christians is still not inconsiderable with whom it is a principal article of belief, that the Eternal God has been so united to a man as to form one person—opinions, which are alike inconsistent with the doctrine of the immensity of the Divine nature: for it is most evidently impossible, that the great Being, who is every where, should be of an human form, or should be inclosed in a human body.

This

This doctrine may be farther applied to expose the folly of polytheism and idolatry. If God be essentially present in every part of the universe, it necessarily follows that there is but one God, and that there is no likeness of him either in heaven above or in earth beneath. Since God who made the world, and all things therein, fills heaven and earth with his presence; since in him all creatures live and move, and have their being; men certainly ought not to think, that the Godhead is like unto gold, or silver, graven by art and man's device; nor could any thing be more absurd than that idolatrous worship, which confounded imaginary deities, the gods of the hills and of the valleys, the woods and of the seas, with the God of the universe.

Another important use which may be made of this doctrine is, to convince us of the reasonableness of religious worship,

ship, and of the necessity of worshipping God in spirit and in truth.

If God be present in every part of the universe, in all the excellencies of his nature, there can be no place where he is not a fit object of worship; nor any of his rational offspring, which are not bound to express their veneration and gratitude towards him in acts of devotion. The God whom we worship is no local deity, presiding over a particular region or country, but the God of universal nature. He is not more truly present in the most magnificent temple, in the most numerous assembly, or even in the most glorious celestial regions, than in the humblest cottage or the most solitary retreat. The Eternal God dwelleth not in temples made with hands: in every place his eyes are upon the righteous, and his ears are open to their prayers. He can, without difficulty, at the same instant, hear, approve, and accept the service,

vice, which is paid him by all the worshipping assemblies upon the face of the earth; receive the homage of all his rational offspring through every part of his immense creation. We may join to present our sincere and humble devotions unto him, with as firm an assurance of being heard and accepted, as if we were uniting with angels and the spirits of just men made perfect in the exalted services of the heavenly state. Nay every individual may be assured, that when he prays to his Father in secret, he who seeth in secret, will reward him openly.

How rational, and, at the same time, how solemn, do the exercises of religion appear, when considered as immediately addressed to that glorious Being who is alike present in every place! What can be more natural and fit, than that we should assemble to offer up our praises and prayers to the Great Author of our being, the bountiful giver of all our enjoyments, and the sovereign disposer of our lot, who

who is always with us to hear and accept of our devotions! With what sacred awe should we pay our homage to our Maker, since we cannot doubt, that *he* is as truly present with us as our fellow worshippers! In the performance of these sacred duties, when we find ourselves negligent or languid, let us recall our attention, and awaken our devotion, by saying, " Surely God is in this place, and I knew it not."

The doctrine of the Divine omnipresence and omniscience, may be farther applied as a powerful motive to abstain from every vice, and to live in the sincere and steady practice of all virtue. Hypocritical pretensions to piety, my brethren, can at best only impose upon our fellow-creatures: the Almighty cannot be deceived: his eye pierceth through the thickest veil: he looks within us, and reads our hearts. It is therefore as foolish as it is criminal, to attempt to conceal base designs and corrupt passions under the mask of extraordinary sanctity. Let us then be above all things careful, that in religion we do not substitute the appearance instead of the reality, the shadow instead of the substance. Whilst we assume the form of godliness, let us take heed that we be not strangers to the power.

There is no darkness nor shadow of death, where the workers of iniquity may hide themselves from the presence of God.

Our actions lie as open to the Divine inspection, in the thickest midnight darkness, as in the full blaze of the meridian sun. Men may retire from the world to practise the "hidden things of dishonesty" and wickedness: but there is no recess into which they can retire from the Almighty: "He compasseth our path, and is acquainted with all our ways." No action, no word, no sentiment, can be concealed from his observation.

"His

"His eyes are upon all the ways of the sons of men, to give to every one according to his ways, and according to the fruit of his doings."

Consider this, ye that forget God; ye that prophane his name, and violate his laws. Let the man, who takes advantage of his neighbour's ignorance to practise upon him the arts of deceit, or of his weakness, to oppress and injure him; let the man, who in secret dares to plunder the fatherless and widow, to betray his trust, or to commit actions which he would have been afraid or ashamed to expose to the public eye, remember that there is an eye which he cannot escape; that he is seen and condemned by a Being who is too wise and righteous to connive at iniquity, and who hath declared, that though hand join in hand, the wicked shall not go unpunished. If the worst of men are under some kind of restraint in the presence of persons eminent ment for wisdom and goodness, what a powerful check would it be upon all criminal actions, could men be universally engaged to consider themselves as in the presence of the Almighty, and in every season of temptation to reflect, "How shall I do this great wickedness and sin against God?"—On the other hand, what greater encouragement to uprightness and integrity can be supposed, than a firm persuasion of the immediate and perpetual presence of "the righteous Lord, who loveth righteousness?" If the hope of gaining the esteem of wise and good men inspires every generous mind with a desire of excelling, what may not be expected from the noble ambition of being approved and honoured by the Supreme Judge and rewarder of merit?—Let this important truth then, so frequently employ our meditations, as to become to us a constant and powerful spring of action, that under its influence we may abstain from every vice and cultivate every virtue.

Lastly, Having secured the approbation of the Almighty by living in all good conscience before him, let us derive, from the doctrine of his universal presence, comfort under all the changes and troubles of human life. God, the eternal guardian and friend of the righteous, is ever near unto them, to do them good: his power is their support, his wisdom their guide, and his goodness their consolation. Whatever afflictions befall them, they may be assured that they are not forsaken by that great Being, who can cause all things to work together for good. In whatever part of the world their lot may be cast, they are still under the protection of God: if they go beyond the utmost sea, even there will his hand lead them, and " his right hand uphold them." If it should ever happen, that their character should be traduced, their
sincerity

sincerity questioned, and their actions and motives misrepresented: if it should even happen that they should be defamed and persecuted for their adherence to truth and to conscience, they may support themselves under this painful trial by reflecting, that the Almighty sees and approves their conduct. In the thickest gloom of adversity, when they are least able to discern the wisdom and kindness of the Divine appointments concerning them, and are ready to say, with Job, "Behold, I go forward, but he is not there, and backward, but I cannot perceive him; on the left hand, where he doth work, but I cannot behold him; he hideth himself on the right hand, that I cannot see him:" even at such seasons the upright and virtuous may console themselves with the thought, that they are in the presence, and under the direction of the wisest and best of Beings, who, in the darkest dispensations of his providence, is pursuing the most merciful designs. Let those, then, whose hearts are upright before God, suppress their fears and banish their cares, and, through an humble faith in his ever present aid, endure with patience and fortitude the burdens of mortality. Under all the evils which they either suffer or apprehend, let them say, " God is my refuge and strength, a present help in trouble; therefore will not I fear, though the earth be removed, and though the mountains be carried into the midst of the sea;"—" I have set the Lord always before me; because he is at my right-hand, I shall not be moved."

On the Faithfulnefs of God.

Deuteronomy vii. 9.

Know therefore that the Lord thy God, he is God, the FAITHFUL *God.*

Under whatever afpect the moral character of the Supreme Being is contemplated, it is adapted to excite the emotions of pious reverence, and to afford important inftruction. And fince all the moral perfections which we afcribe to the Deity, if they mean any thing at all, muft denote qualities fimilar in their nature, though infinitely fuperior in degree, to the correfpondent excellencies in man, we have fufficient ground for reprefenting him before our minds under all the varieties of attribute, which we can conceive

ceive to be comprehended in the general idea of absolute perfection.

One essential branch of human goodness, without which we cannot suppose the character of a virtuous man complete, is veracity, or faithfulness; a virtue which consists in an exact correspondence between the conceptions of the mind, and the expressions, whatever they be, by which these conceptions are communicated. By a man of veracity, we mean one, whose words are a plain declaration of his mind, and whose actions agree with the assurances he has given. And we think it necessary to complete this character, not only that a man's declarations be literally true, and his promises be in some sense fulfilled, but that both correspond to the ideas, or expectations, which he intended to raise.

That this quality may be conceived to belong to the Supreme Being, no one will doubt, who reflects for a moment upon the various ways in which he declares his purposes

purposes and will to mankind. By forming different beings with different capacities, and placing them in different situations, he has prescribed to each order their respective objects of pursuit and methods of acting; whence the law of their nature becomes to them the law of God. Among rational beings, wherever the Great Ruler has established a manifest connexion between any course of action and certain consequences, whether agreeable or painful, he has herein shewn his pleasure that such a course of action should be pursued or avoided; and this settled order of things, in the moral world, has all the force and obligation of a positive command or prohibition. In like manner, if it has pleased the Supreme Being to raise in the minds of men a persuasion of the Divine authority of any messenger, who professes to be sent from God, and to confirm that persuasion by sufficient testimony, the doctrine which such a Divine messenger delivers is unquestionably

questionably to be received as a manifestation of the Divine will. In all these cases, we may as justly consider the Almighty as making declarations to mankind, as if he were to speak to them by an audible voice from heaven. And, since, in these communications, the Deity must necessarily be either true and faithful, or otherwise, we have sufficient ground for at least conceiving of him under the character of the Faithful God. And that this character does in fact belong to him, is a point which it will by no means be difficult to establish.

If any thing can be pronounced with certainty respecting the Divine nature, it is surely this, that it must be superior in excellence to human nature, and therefore cannot partake of the imperfections of human beings. Now every one must be sensible, that there is no quality which is more disgraceful even to human nature than a propensity to falsehood. Why is it universally esteemed

the

the highest indignity that can be offered to any man to give him the lie, but because a disposition to lying is always regarded as an indication of a base and servile spirit? And shall that which is contemptible among men, be imputed to that Being who is the standard of excellence, and the source of all perfection? The supposition is as absurd, as the assertion would be impious.

We may, moreover, infer this moral attribute of the Divine nature from those natural perfections which are manifested in his works. If we could suppose the Deity to deviate from truth or to violate his word, it must be from some cause or motive which cannot exist in a Being possessed of uncontroulable power, perfect knowledge, and unerring wisdom. Men are tempted to falsehood by the apprehension of incurring some evil, or the desire of obtaining some benefit: but Omnipotence cannot fear, and Infinite Perfection cannot hope. With respect to promises,

promises, if we could suppose the Supreme Being to fail in accomplishing these, it must either be through inconsideration and precipitancy in making them, through forgetfulness after they are made, through inconstancy and fickleness, or through the want of power. Besides these, no other causes of the violation of a promise can be conceived. But none of these can possibly subsist in the Divine mind. A Being, perfect in wisdom, can never promise any thing which would be unfit, or ever wish to change his purpose; an omniscient Being can never fail to accomplish his purpose through inattention; and a Being possessed of omnipotence cannot be at a loss for means to execute his designs and engagements.

It is wholly unnecessary to advance further arguments on so clear a point; on the principles which have been laid down, we may admit it as a certain truth, that the Lord our God is a faithful God. " God is not a man, that he should

should lie; nor the son of man, that he should repent: hath he said, and will he not do it? hath he spoken, and will he not make it good? He will not suffer his faithfulness to fail; nor alter the thing which is gone out of his lips."

If any expressions occur in the holy scriptures, which may seem to contradict this doctrine, there can be no doubt that they ought to be, and it will commonly be found, that they easily may be explained in a manner perfectly consistent with it. When God is said, in the prophecy of Jonah, to have repented him of the evil with which he had threatened Nineveh, we are to understand the expressions as intimating, not that he failed to execute his threatening through inconstancy, but that the threatening having been in its nature conditional, when the Ninevites through their repentance ceased to be proper objects of punishment, the sentence against them was reversed.

To obviate every difficulty upon this subject,

subject, it is only necessary to consider the nature of a threatening as the sanction of a law, intended to intimate what is to be expected, if the offence against which it is directed be committed. The threatening does indeed suppose, that, if the offence take place, the punishment will follow; and it would be an impeachment of the veracity of the Supreme Lawgiver, and would seem to defeat the ends of the Divine government, to suppose that the threatened punishment would, in any case, not be inflicted upon impenitent offenders. But since the end of threatening is not the infliction, but the prevention of punishment, the threatening may, without any impeachment of veracity, be reversed, when the crime against which it is denounced is either not committed, or is sincerely repented of. The Divine threatenings are to be understood in the conditional sense in which the prophet Jeremiah represents them: " At what instant I shall speak concerning a nation, and

and concerning a kingdom, to pluck up, and to pull down, and to deftroy it; if that nation againſt whom I have pronounced turn from their evil ways, then will I repent of the evil that I thought to do them."

Having thus eſtabliſhed the doctrine of the Divine faithfulneſs, and obviated the objections which might ſeem to lie againſt it, let us proceed to the practical improvement of the important and delightful truth, that the Lord our God is a faithful God.

And, firſt, we ſhould learn from the doctrine of the text to confide, with perfect aſſurance, in the Divine declarations and promiſes.

Since our Almighty Creator is a being of perfect veracity, we may aſſure ourſelves, that whatever he hath clearly taught, whether by the conſtitution of human nature, by the eſtabliſhed order of providence, or by expreſs revelation, is unqueſtionably true. If it be admitted, as we have seen that we have the cleareſt reaſons for admitting, that God cannot intend to deceive his creatures, it muſt follow, that we may ſafely rely upon the report of our ſenſes and feelings, examined and corrected by the underſtanding which God hath given us; and that, if we are impoſed upon in things which concern our well-being, it is through precipitancy and prejudice, and not through any defect in the conſtitution of our nature. In like manner, in whatever other ways the Almighty hath ſpoken to us, whether in the ordinary diſpenſations of his providence, or by divine inſtructors, who have been appointed to enlighten the world, we ſhould receive his communications with entire confidence, firmly perſuaded that *his word is truth.*

We may alſo conclude, from the doctrine of the divine veracity, that whatever expectations the Almighty has raiſed by the ſtructure of the human mind, by the eſtabliſhed courſe of events, or by expreſs revelation,

revelation, will be accomplished. Every expectation raised in this manner may justly be considered in the light of a *promise*, or covenant; and those blessings which God promises to his creatures are justly stiled in Scripture *sure mercies*; for the accomplishment is secured by the eternal and immutable perfections of his nature. In our expectations from our fellow-creatures, however reasonable, we may possibly be disappointed; for they are fallible and mutable. But the promise of God is sure: his covenant standeth fast for ever. " Know ye, that the Lord thy God, he is God, a faithful God, who keepeth covenant and mercy with them that love him, and keep his commandments, to a thousand generations."

Let the pious servants of God hold fast their confidence in God without wavering; for he is faithful who hath promised. Let neither the appearance of improbability, nor the delay or distance of accomplishment, lead you to entertain a doubt of the performance of the Divine promises.

Has he encouraged you to hope, that he will in the issue cause all things to work together for good to those who love him? Let not present gloomy appearances lead you to distrust the kindness of his designs. What though you may be at present surrounded with difficulties, from which you can see no way of escape; and oppressed with afflictions, which seem almost too heavy for human nature to support; let not your heart be cast down, or your spirit be disquieted within you: but still hope in God; for you shall yet praise him who is the health of your countenance, and your God. Remember, that his thoughts are not as our thoughts, nor his ways as our ways; but that as the heavens are high above the earth, so are his thoughts and ways above ours: and that though his judgments are unsearchable, and his ways past finding out, righteousness and mercy are the everlasting
foundations

foundations of his throne. In all your troubles caſt your care upon him, with a firm perſuaſion that he careth for you; and that, though many are the afflictions of the righteous, the Lord will deliver him out of them all.

Are we taught by the goſpel of Chriſt to expect a reſurrection from the dead; and aſſured by our Saviour, who ſpake to mankind in the name of God, that all who are in their graves ſhall hear the voice of the Son of Man, and ſhall come forth? Let us not ſuppoſe it an impoſſible thing, that they who are ſleeping in the duſt of the earth ſhould be called to life, and crowned with immortal vigour. Have we not heard, have we not known, that the everlaſting God, the Lord, the Creator of the ends of the earth, fainteth not, neither is weary! Why ſhould we doubt, that he who firſt formed the body of man out of the duſt of the ground, can at the reſurrection give him a body as he pleaſes? Shall it be thought a thing incredible, that he who brought the vaſt and goodly ſyſtem of nature into being, and who breathed into man the breath of life, ſhould raiſe the dead? Inſtead of preſuming to ſet bounds to Omnipotence, and to ſay to the Moſt High—" Hitherto canſt thou go, but no further;" let us confide in the aſſurances of the goſpel, that this corruptible ſhall hereafter put on incorruption, and this mortal put on immortality.

Hath God, who cannot lie, promiſed us eternal life through Jeſus Chriſt our Lord? Let no falſe notions of the meanneſs of human nature on the one hand; nor any exalted conceptions of the vaſt felicity which muſt be included in an immortal happy exiſtence, on the other, incline us to doubt concerning the completion of the promiſe. Our future happineſs is not to be limited by our deſerts, but is to proceed from the free favour and rich bounty of God, whoſe mercy is everlaſting upon them that fear him. Why ſhould we we entertain a doubt, that the same Divine Power which at first brought us into being, and which continually upholds us in life, can sustain us in existence, through any the most distant period of future duration? or that the same goodness which induces him to make us happy at present, will incline him to preserve us in being, and perpetuate our happiness, throughout eternity? Since our Maker hath instamped upon our minds, in their intellectual and moral capacities, an image of his own eternal nature; and since he hath sent his son Jesus Christ into the world to bring life and immortality to light; let us confide in the promise of eternal life as a faithful saying, and give all diligence to prepare ourselves for that felicity, to the hope of which the God of all grace hath called us.

Be it, however, remembered, that we are not so far to presume upon the promise of God, as to imagine that it will be fulfilled with respect to any of us, if we neglect to comply with the condition of the promife. "If thou wilt enter into life," faith our Saviour, "keep the commandments." This is the indifpenfable condition of the Chriftian covenant: and no man, who refufes to comply with fo reafonable a requifition, can have any juft ground to complain that God is unfaithful in denying him the bleffing which he has promifed only to the righteous. Nay, it may be added, that the Divine veracity itfelf precludes the expectation of future happinefs on any other terms; for the fame voice which hath promifed glory, honour, and immortality, to every man that worketh good, hath alfo denounced indignation and wrath, tribulation and anguifh, upon every foul of man that worketh evil: and we have no right to queftion the threatening, more than the promife, of Omnipotence. Although the Lord be long fuffering to us-ward, not willing that any fhould perifh, but that all fhould come to the knowledge of the truth, the day of juft retribution will come,

come, in which the wicked will be doomed to everlasting destruction. Wherefore, beloved, seeing that ye look for such things, be diligent, that ye may be found of your Judge in peace, without spot, and blameless; and having conscientiously endeavoured to keep the commandments of God, live in the joyful expectation of the promised felicity. Under all the troubles of this life, let the promise of eternal happiness afford you good hope and strong consolation; and in the hour of death commit your spirits into the hands of your merciful and faithful Creator, looking for the blessed hope and the glorious appearing of the great God, and of our Saviour Jesus Christ.

Lastly, let us learn, from the doctrine of the Divine faithfulness, to be ourselves true and faithful both towards God and man.

An appeal to Heaven by an oath appears peculiarly solemn, when it is considered, that in this act of religion we call the God of truth to atteſt that we ſpeak the truth. It is impoſſible to conceive any obligation more ſacred than this; nor any higher indignity which can be offered to the Supreme Being than perjury. But it is not merely in an oath that we bind ourſelves to truth and faithfulneſs towards our Maker, but in every pious reſolution and purpoſe which we form in his preſence. Whether we voluntarily take upon ourſelves the profeſſion of religion in the ordinances of Chriſtianity, or in ſolemn acts of devotion declare our deſire and determination to obey the will of God, we ought to conſider theſe external acts of religion as a ſolemn promiſe, by which we acknowledge our aſſent to the eternal law of reaſon, and bind ourſelves to comply with the condition upon which the Divine promiſe of eternal life is ſuſpended. If, after ſuch engagements, we continue to live in the violation of the Divine laws, our diſobedience becomes unfaithfulneſs, and involves us in aggravated guilt. Let us, us, then, remember the vows of God which are upon us, and say with the pious Psalmist—" I have sworn, and I will perform it, that I will keep all God's righteous judgments."

Let us, moreover, be careful to imitate the Divine veracity in all our transactions with each other. It is an essential part of the character of the good man, that if he sweareth to his own hurt, he changeth not. The law of truth is in his heart, and deceit and falsehood have no place in his words. What he thinks, he speaks; what he promises, he performs. That we may the more easily discharge this part of our duty, we should be careful not to enter into any engagements which we cannot fulfil without subjecting ourselves to great, and otherwise unnecessary, inconvenience. But having bound ourselves by a solemn promise, we are under indispensable obligations to execute it faithfully, in all cases which would not imply a violation of the prior obligations of moral duty.

In fine, if we wish to become followers of the God of truth, we must in all our devotions worship him in sincerity and in truth; sincerely intending that obedience to his will which we profess ourselves resolved to maintain: in the whole of our lives we must steadily adhere to the pious resolutions and purposes we express in our prayers; and in our daily intercourse with each other we must refrain from every kind of falsehood and dissimulation; faithfully execute every trust; strictly adhere to our engagements; and, in all things, obey that eternal law of truth which is the rule by which the actions of all good beings, even of God himself, are directed. "Lie not one to another," saith the apostle Paul, "seeing that ye have put off the old man with his deeds, and have put on the new man, which is renewed in knowledge after the image of him that created him."

Characters of the Works of God.

Revelation xv. 3.

Great and marvellous are thy works, Lord God Almighty.

It is to be regretted, that so much of the impression which the grandeur and beauty of nature are adapted to make upon our minds, is prevented or effaced by familiarity. The magnificent scenery of the material world first presents itself to our senses, at a period of life when we are incapable of reflection; and afterwards opens upon our understandings in such detached portions, and by such slow gradations, as almost entirely to preclude the lively emotions of surprise and admiration. Hence we are too apt to wander

der over the well-known objects around us, however grand and sublime, however beautiful, or however instructive, with the vacant eye of inattention. Whilst Nature is perpetually proclaiming, through all her works, that there is a Power above us, and that the Being who made and governs all things, is great and wise, and good, beyond our most exalted conceptions, we are too often inclined to receive her report with the carelessness and coldness with which we hear an old and worn-out tale.

To compensate, in some measure, for the inconvenience which unavoidably arises from the frequency with which the objects of nature come under the notice of our senses, without leading our minds to the contemplation of its great Author, it is necessary that we sometimes make it our deliberate and serious business to survey the world in which we dwell as the workmanship of the Lord God Almighty. We should contemplate the ordinary appearances

pearances of grandeur and beauty in the heavens and the earth, not merely to afford an elegant entertainment to the imagination, or to gratify a refined and cultivated taste, but to fix in our minds a deep and habitual impression of those sentiments of veneration and gratitude, with which the Intelligent Source of all that is great and good ought ever to be regarded.

It is one of the greatest advantages which we derive from the advancement of natural knowledge, that by giving us more extensive and accurate views of nature in its several departments, it furnishes us with innumerable illustrations of the power, the wisdom, and the goodness, of the Supreme Being, which are wholly unknown to vulgar or uninformed minds, and consequently tends to correct and elevate our conceptions of him, whom, after our utmost exertions, we shall never find out to perfection. To content ourselves with merely observing the appearances,

and

and investigating the laws, of the material world, without applying our observations to the purposes of religion, would be to deprive ourselves of one of the most valuable fruits of philosophy. Every object in nature which is adapted to awaken our curiosity, excite our admiration, or afford us pleasure, becomes doubly interesting, when it is contemplated as the work of God. Allow me, then, at this time, to conduct you through a general survey of the material creation under this character, and to lay before you such particulars respecting the *grandeur*, the *beauty*, the *variety*, the *mutual relation*, and the *utility*, of the Divine works, as may serve to strengthen your pious sentiments, and to call from your lips the language of devout admiration—" Great and marvellous are thy works, Lord God Almighty !"

The characters of grandeur and magnificence are so legibly inscribed upon the general face of nature, that the most untaught eye cannot fail to read them, nor
the

the most uncultivated imagination to contemplate them with admiration. The surface of the earth, considered merely as a vast picture drawn by the hand of Nature, exhibits scenes adapted to excite emotions of sublimity. Plains, whose extent exceeds the limits of human vision; mountains whose sides are embrowned with craggy rocks, and whose majestic summits hide themselves in the clouds; seas, whose spreading waters unite far distant countries; and oceans, which begird the vast globe itself, are objects, at all times, striking to the imagination. If from the earth we lift up our eyes on high, new scenes of magnificence demand our attentive admiration: the glorious sun, the eye and soul of this material world, possessing his seat amidst the vast expanse, and spreading light and heat through the world; and, in their turn, the numberless lamps of night illuminating the firmament with their native fires.

Let

Let the great powers of nature be brought into action, and still more sublime and awful appearances rise to our view. Let woods and forests wave before the stormy winds; let Ocean " heave from his extended bed," and roll his threatening billows to the sky; let volcanos pour forth pillars of smoke and melted torrents from their fiery caverns; let lightnings dart their vivid fires through the sky, whilst thunders roar among the bursting clouds; what imagination shall remain unimpressed with emotions of admiration mingled with terror?

A lively sense of grandeur and sublimity is naturally produced by scenes like these, even in uninformed and uncultivated minds. But to the man whom philosophy has taught to penetrate beyond the surface of things, and to discover the principles and laws of nature, the works of God appear still more grand and sublime. Every individual body in nature is considered,

sidered, by the man thus enlightened, as preserved in its form by the uniform action of one power or principle by which its parts are held together. By another universal power, he observes all the bodies upon this earth tending towards its center; and, comparing the laws by which this attracting power is found to operate, with the well-known motions of the heavenly bodies, he finds that this single principle is sufficient to account for these motions; and consequently infers, from analogy, that this power, uniformly exerted, forms the grand chain which unites the several parts of the universe in one system. Hence he derives an inexpressibly sublime conception of that Great Being who is the seat of this principle, and the source of its operation. The man who is thus enlightened by the study of nature, sees this earth as a globe of vast magnitude, moving perpetually round the sun with a degree of rapidity much greater than

than has ever been produced by human force or art: at the same time he sees other globes, some less, and others much larger, than the earth, revolving with inconceivable rapidity round the sun, as their common center, at distances so great that, though they may be expressed in numbers, they far exceed the utmost stretch of the human imagination. This set of planets, which he knows to have, with our earth, a common relation to the sun, he very reasonably concludes to be a system of worlds, all peopled with suitable inhabitants, and all deriving supplies of light and heat from the same source. Extending his views beyond this system, and finding, from observation, that the fixed stars are in themselves luminous bodies, and that their distance from the earth is so much greater than that of the planets or sun, as to be absolutely immeasurable, he concludes, upon the most probable grounds, that those sparkling gems which
deck

deck the robe of night, are not placed in the heavens merely for the convenience of this earth, but are, like our glorious luminary, funs to their refpective fyftems of worlds. And, finally, when by the affiftance of art he is enabled to difcover innumerable ftars hitherto unobferved, he judges that he has better ground than mere conjecture for thinking, that funs and worlds are extended through the immenfe regions of fpace infinitely beyond all human calculation or conception. How fublime the idea! how much are we indebted to that kind of philofophy which has put us in poffeffion of it! efpecially, fince it has not left the great fabric it has difcovered without an inhabitant—fince it has inftructed us, on the cleareft principle of reafon, that of affigning to every effect an adequate caufe, that this immenfe, this glorious univerfe, is the habitation of One Great Being, who framed, who pervades, who animates, who governs

verns the whole! How reasonable is it that this universe, which is the mansion of the Divinity, should be the temple in which all created beings should, in one triumphant chorus, unite to say—" Great and marvellous are thy works, O Lord God Almighty!" Hallelujah! for the Lord God Omnipotent reigneth!

But we must descend from these lofty conceptions, to turn our attention to several other leading characters of the works of God. Of these, that which, next in order, comes under our notice, is *beauty*.

The sentiment by which we are delighted with whatever is beautiful, is not less natural than that by which we admire whatever is grand and sublime; nor has the Author of nature less liberally provided for its gratification. To *illustrate* this part of my subject, I might cull the choicest flowers which Poetry or Painting have gathered from the lap of Nature. I might lead you, in imagination,

through

through some rich and varied landscape, where your eye should be delighted with verdant meads and flowery lawns, and your ear soothed with the murmur of streams, or enchanted with the music of the groves. I might represent before you, in succession, the diversified beauties of cheerful Spring, of fruitful Summer, of plenteous Autumn, and of Winter clothed in her silver robe of snow. I might conduct you through the leading classes of the vegetable and animal world, and call upon you to remark in each the distinct beauties, of colour, form, proportion, animated motion, and grace. But this is a detail which your own imaginations will easily supply. Let it suffice, then, upon this head, to remark, in general, that the colouring of beauty, which is so liberally spread over the productions of nature, are as real, though not perhaps such striking, proofs of the power, wisdom, and goodness, of the Great Creator, as the lines of grandeur and sublimity; and that, therefore, we ought not to overlook his hand in the former more than in the latter. If we may be allowed to apply the language of human arts to the works of God, we may truly say, that whilst the great conception of the Almighty Artist appears in the grand outline of nature, *his* " pencil also glows in every flower." Whilst, therefore, we find an elegant and most laudable amusement, in studying or imitating the beauties of nature, let us sometimes raise a thought of admiration and gratitude to him who hath created every thing "beautiful in its season." To those who, whilst they are ambitious of cultivating a taste for whatever is sublime or beautiful in the productions of nature or of art, forget the first Source of beauty and of skill, the forcible and elegant language of the Author of the Book of Wisdom may be properly applied— " Surely vain are all men by nature who

are

are ignorant of God, and could not, out of the things that are feen, know him that is: neither by confidering the works, did they acknowledge the Work-mafter; but deemed either fire, or wind, or the fwift air, or the circle of the ftars, or the violent water, or the lights of heaven, to be the gods which govern the world. With whofe beauty if they, being delighted, took them to be gods, let them know how much better the Lord of them is: for the firft Author of beauty hath created them; or, if they were aftonifhed at *their power* and virtue, let them underftand by them, how much mightier he is that made them. For by the greatnefs and beauty of the creatures, proportionally the Maker of them is feen.

The variety which appears in nature, is the offspring, not of confufion, but of order. Though the forms of individual beings are infinitely diverfified, fo that it is perhaps impoffible to find, in the whole

compass of nature, two organized bodies perfectly alike, yet, amidst this boundless variety, we may observe the most perfect regularity. This regularity is of two kinds, that of *gradation*, and that of *arrangement*. That of gradation chiefly appears in *animated nature*, where beings possess different powers and faculties through a long succession, each holding his proper place in the scale of excellence. That of *arrangement* prevails through the whole visible world; each individual possessing some qualities or characters, in common with some others, which enable the spectator to consider them as belonging to the same species or kind; and each species partaking with some others of common appearances, by means of which they may be classed under some general description; till, at length, we arrive at the three comprehensive divisions, under which all the bodies which belong to this earth are commonly arranged, animals, vegetables, and minerals. Under which-
soever

foever of thefe views we contemplate the objects around us, we muft be ftruck with the perception of that pleafure which arifes from regulated variety. If we attempt to trace the fcale of life, in this world, from the fhell-fifh, which is fixed to the fpot which produced it, and appears to poffefs no other fenfe than that of feeling, through all the ftages of exiftence, rifing one above another, by fteps fcarcely perceptible, in their capacities for enjoyment and action, till we reach the human fpecies, to whom Providence hath evidently affigned the firft place on this terreftrial globe: if, from man, we rife in imagination through various orders of intellectual being, till we reach thofe exalted powers who are honoured with the firft ftation beneath the Eternal Throne, what an amazing variety of exiftence, of capacity, of enjoyment, fhall we find in paffing from nothing to man— from man to God! Or if, availing ourfelves of the obfervations of naturalifts upon the animal, vegetable, and mineral kingdoms, we become acquainted with the several classes of beasts and birds, and fishes, and insects, of trees and shrubs, of metals and stones, earths and waters, which are found and described among the productions of nature upon the face of this globe, how shall we be struck with astonishment at the survey! If withal we contemplate these varieties in nature as resulting from the inexhaustible contrivance and unerring skill of one great Artificer, what abundant cause shall we find for saying, O Lord, how manifold are thy works! in wisdom thou hast made them all!

Amidst the boundless variety of the works of God, let it also be considered, as another character by which they are distinguished, that there every-where subsists between them a mutual *connection* and *dependence*.

The law of mutual dependence so universally

universally prevails, that through all the parts of nature which come under our notice, and probably throughout the creation, there is not to be found a single infulated, unconnected, being. It is true, in numberlefs inftances, that the parts of the material world are dependent upon each other for their prefervation. The nourifhment of plants is the joint labour of the fun and air, earth and water; and even the continuance of their feveral fpecies requires that plants of the fame order be affociated in the fame foil. Animals depend upon vegetables, or upon animals of an inferior fize or lower order, for their fupport; and in their refpective claffes are often mutually fubfervient to each other. Man, the lord of this lower creation, requires large fupplies from the vegetable, animal, and mineral kingdoms, for his fupport, defence, convenience, and amufement; and in return is under the neceffity of cultivating the earth, and of

protecting

protecting and providing for the creatures whofe fervices he needs. Among men, every relation of fociety is a mode of dependence, and all the offices of focial life are reciprocal acts of kindnefs. As in the human body, the eye cannot fay to the hand, I have no need of thee, nor again, the head, I have no need of you; fo in the general body of fociety, no individual can claim independence on his brethren. " None of us liveth to himfelf." In fine, the whole material world appears to be one general fyftem, all the parts of which are held together by one common law of attraction; and the whole intellectual world may be juftly confidered as one vaft fociety, the members of which are reciprocally united by the common bond of benevolence. Thus are all the creatures of God bound to each other by the chain of mutual dependence. And let us not forget to add, that the firft link of this chain is faftened

to

to the footstool of the Almighty's throne. "Of him are all things, and by him all things subsist."

The last character of the works of God, to which I shall at present direct your thoughts, is UTILITY.

If the value of every work depends upon the importance of the end it is designed to answer, and the degree of perfection with which it accomplishes that end, the works of God are glorious and excellent, and, to say all in one word, worthy of their Author. The best design which can be conceived is that of producing happiness. The most exalted conception which can be supposed to enter into the Divine mind is that of blessing a universe. This vast and exalted design is written in legible characters upon the whole face of nature. Every intelligent, every percipient being, is, by the structure of his frame and the faculties with which he is endued, created for happiness. Abundant provision is made

in

in the material world, and in the general nature and tendencies of things for producing universal felicity. We may therefore reasonably presume, that every occurrence which seems at present to interrupt this great design, is only a temporary appearance, which, for want of seeing the whole extent of the Divine plan, we cannot explain, and that all *partial evil* will terminate in *universal good*. Consequently, when we observe the great operations of nature affording life, convenience, enjoyment, to the numerous inhabitants of the world, we may, without hesitation, conclude, the works of God to be, in the noblest and most perfect sense of the term, *useful*. When we observe, that the eye is formed for seeing, and the ear for hearing, that every sense and every faculty has its proper enjoyment, and that nature is a vast store-house, richly furnished with every thing to gratify the senses, and to diffuse contentment and gladness through the

the heart, we ought to infer concerning the works of God, not only that they are executed with infinite skill, but they are wisely adapted to accomplish the purposes of infinite benevolence. It is not only true that God hath made all things for their use, but that " every creature of God is good."

After this survey of the leading characters of the works of God, which of us will not be disposed to adopt with devout admiration the language of our Divine Poet:

These are thy glorious works, Parent of good!
Almighty! thine, this universal frame,
Thus wondrous fair! thyself how wondrous then!
Unspeakable! who sit'st above these heavens
To us invisible, or dimly seen
In these thy lowest works: yet these declare
Thy goodness beyond thought and power Divine!

Study the works of nature for a higher purpose than merely to furnish you with an amusing employment for your leisure hours, or with fruitful topics of entertaining

taining conversation. Let philosophy conduct you to the temple of religion. Contemplate the objects and productions of nature as the great and marvellous works of Almighty God. And let the contemplation confirm your faith in his Being and Providence, exalt your conceptions of his nature, and lead you not to look up to him with superstitious terror, or to approach him with fanatical familiarity or mystical enthusiasm, but, at all times, to think and to speak of him, and to worship him, with all reverence as THE FIRST BEING IN THE UNIVERSE.

Glory be to God for ever! Amen.

The Christian Religion, a valuable Treasure.

MATTHEW xiii. 44.

The kingdom of heaven is like unto treasure hid in a field; which, when a man hath found, he hideth, and for joy thereof, goeth and selleth all that he hath and buyeth that field.

In the preceding parables, recorded in this chapter, our Saviour had described the different reception which his doctrine would meet with from men of different characters: foretold the mixture of good and bad men which should afterwards be found in his church, and the separation which should finally be made

made between them; and reprefented the future fpread of his gofpel, from the fmalleft beginnings, till it fhould extend its influence and authority through the world. He proceeds, in this parable, to inftruct his difciples, that the religion which he was about to eftablifh would be an ineftimable bleffing to mankind. This point he illuftrates by two fimilitudes. He firft compares the kingdom of heaven, or the Chriftian religion, to a treafure hid in a field, which, when a man hath found, he keeps fecret, and with great delight goes and fells all he poffeffes, and buys the field. He next compares it to a precious gem or pearl, which a merchant, who goes abroad in fearch of fuch treafures, having met with an opportunity of purchafing on advantageous terms, fells whatever he has, that he may become poffeffed of it. The points of refemblance between the principal object and the fecondary of thefe parables are two: firft, the value of the treafure; and

and, secondly, the earnest desire of the person by whom it is discovered, to make it his own. Like the treasure spoken of in the former simile, and like the goodly pearl in the latter, the gospel of Christ, or the doctrine which he hath taught, is a possession of inestimable worth, which cannot be too dearly purchased. And, as in both the cases supposed, the person who made the fortunate discovery, did not hesitate to part with all his former possessions, in order to make the treasure he had discovered his own, so a wise man, who perceives the importance of the Christian religion to the reformation, improvement, and happiness, of mankind, and is sensible that the blessings which it promises are infinitely superior in value to any thing which this world can bestow, will think no labour, hazard, or sacrifice, too great, in order to furnish himself with the present advantages which it affords, and to secure to himself the future felicities which it reveals. Let us confider the parables in both thefe points of view, to ftrengthen our conviction of the value of our Chriftian privileges, and to excite us to the utmoft diligence in improving them.

The gofpel of Chrift, or that divine religion which was taught by our Saviour, and of which the books of the New Teftament are a faithful record, is a rich treafure of truth, of wifdom, of confolation.

Firft, The Gofpel is a rich treafure of truth.

Our Divine Inftructor did not indeed undertake to gratify the vain curiofity of idle fpeculatifts, much lefs to fettle the perverfe difputings of men of " corrupt minds." He paid no attention to many of thofe abftrufe queftions which had baffled the penetration of wife men in all preceding ages ; he took no pains to determine which of the numerous fects of philofophers, which the pride of rea-

foning

soning had created, stood upon the surest ground. He did not even attempt to enlighten the world on subjects of real importance, which had no immediate connexion with morals, or to correct errors of prejudices which did not affect the conduct of life: to improve the arts and sciences, or to establish a new school of philosophy, came not within the limits of his office. But his commission as a teacher sent from God had a much *higher* object; which was, to enlighten the human understanding with that knowledge which would furnish men with solid principles of right conduct, and serve as a lamp to guide their feet into the path of happiness. To render human beings such as nature dictates, and the great Author of nature intends, nothing can be of so much importance as that they should form just ideas of their own faculties, situation, and expectations, and worthy conceptions of their Almighty Creator. Now this great design is most successfully

successfully accomplished in the doctrine of Christ.

The idea which Christianity instructs us to entertain concerning human nature is, that it consists of body and mind, each of which has its respective powers and enjoyments; that the appetites of the former are much inferior in dignity to the capacities of the latter; that the pleasures arising from the indulgence of the one can bear no comparison, either in value or permanency, to the satisfactions and delights which flow from the exercise of the other; that man is endued with social affections, which render the habits of benevolence and generosity essential to his happiness; that he is capable of the sublime conceptions and emotions of genuine piety, and consequently that his happiness must depend in a great measure upon the sentiments which he cherishes with respect to the Supreme Being; and, lastly, that his nature, and consequently his pursuits, are

eminently

eminently distinguished from those of the other inhabitants of this world, by a capacity and expectation of living hereafter, and ever enjoying an immortal existence. These are the ideas of human nature, which, though not established by a formal course of reasoning after the manner of philosophers, are every where supposed to be true, and taken for granted as the natural ground of the several precepts which inculcate the exercise of the social and religious affections, and which prescribe the practice of every moral virtue, as the only means of rendering us happy both in this life and the next.

Christianity also teacheth us the most important truths concerning the nature, perfections, and government, of God. It represents him to us as an invisible and spiritual Being, the Author of all existence and happiness, himself immutable, eternal, and independent; as the supreme Director of all events, without whose providence

providence not even a sparrow falleth to the ground; as the moral Governor of the world, under whose inspection the sons of men are continually acting, and before whose tribunal they must finally appear to receive the reward of their deeds; and, lastly, as the benevolent Father of his creatures, who bountifully dispenses the blessings of his providence even among the unworthy, and who exercises compassion towards the wretched, and lenity towards the guilty. The characters which the Gospel ascribes to the Deity are such as these: the ever-blessed God, who only hath immortality; the Lord Almighty; the only wise God, to whom all his works are known from the beginning of the world; of whom are all things; from whom cometh every good and perfect gift; who giveth us rain from heaven and fruitful seasons; who granteth his holy spirit to them that ask him; whose commandments are not grievous; all whose ways are just and true: with whom

whom is no respect of persons; whose sun shineth upon the evil and upon the good; who is long suffering and merciful, not willing that any one should perish; and, in one word, who is "*love.*"

These truths, both respecting God and man, are, it is owned, discoverable, and were in some measure discovered, by the natural powers of the human mind. But every one who is at all acquainted with the numerous errors in opinion, and the consequent follies and absurdities in practice, which prevailed even in the more enlightened parts of the heathen world, will perceive it to have been a matter of great importance, an object worthy of Divine interposition, that mankind should be clearly and plainly instructed in these important truths. But the value of these treasures of moral and Divine truth will be still more apparent, if it be considered that just principles are the foundation of right conduct, and that it is only where men reverence the Divine nature as the centre and source of all perfection, and respect human nature as an image of the Divine, that they can be expected to support a character worthy of the rational offspring of God.

The Gospel of Christ is, in the second place, richly stored with treasures of practical WISDOM. It abounds with wise precepts and rules for the government of our dispositions and manners, by the diligent observance of which men may be making continual advances towards perfection. The duties which Christianity requires us to perform are such as arise from our nature and condition as men; such as imply an imitation of the Divine excellencies; such as tend to improve our faculties, exalt our characters, and promote our happiness; such, consequently, as must approve themselves to the reason and judgment of every wise man. The laws of our holy religion are adapted to promote the outward prosperity, and the inward peace of individuals, and

and to support the good order, and advance the most important interests of society. They enjoin nothing unnecessary or burdensome; they omit nothing which is reasonable or useful; they restrain us from nothing which would not be contrary to our true interest.

Let any one distinctly examine the laws of Christianity, with a view to remark their natural influence upon personal and social happiness, and he will be at no loss to discover upon them the evident characters of wisdom. Who does not perceive, that the strict observance of those precepts which require us to be sober, chaste, and temperate, "to walk in the spirit and not fulfil the lusts of the flesh," to be pure in heart, to take heed that we offend not in word, "to clothe ourselves with humility, to be diligent in business, and to be contented with such things as we have," must be the surest means of preserving to us the blessings of health, prosperity, a fair reputation,

and

and a peaceful mind? Who can doubt that by "rendering to all their due," "speaking every man truth to his neighbour," doing to others as we would that they should do to us; "loving our neighbour as ourselves, and being ready to do every good work," we most effectually provide for the gratification of the best feelings of our own hearts, most powerfully arrest the esteem and love of all the honest and good around us, and consequently, most certainly lay up in store for ourselves a fund of pleasing reflections and of reasonable expectations against a future day of adversity? Lastly, What mind, which is not an entire stranger to religious ideas and sentiments, can question, whether the pious christian, who in obedience to the precepts of his Divine Master, loves the Lord his God with all his heart and soul, and mind and strength, worships him in spirit and in truth, and commits himself to him in the way of well-doing, experiences a kind of satisfaction

tion and delight in religious contemplation and in acts of devotion, which enable him to say with the Psalmist, " It is good for me to draw near to God!"

Besides these personal advantages which arise from obedience to the laws of Christ, many important benefits accrue hence to society. Christianity, in enjoining all those virtues which tend to meliorate men's temper, and restrain their passions, tears up by the root those weeds which are most destructive of the precious fruits of peace and good-will. By requiring us to love our neighbour, and even our enemies, it discovers itself to be not only the most inoffensive, but the most benevolent institution in the world. By restraining all those unruly passions which tend to disturb the peace of society, and to alienate men from one another; by prohibiting violence and oppression, fraud, perfidy and treachery, and even slander, censoriousness, and ill-nature; and by enforcing the natural dictates of the human heart

Judge, before whom the workers of iniquity cannot stand, the Christian doctrine of Divine mercy sheds a ray of heavenly light over his gloomy prospect, and bids him be of good cheer, for his sins may be forgiven him. The assurance which the gospel affords the sincere penitent, that he shall find mercy, becomes, in such a situation, indeed an inestimable treasure.

Lastly, amidst all the uncertainties of the present world, and in the immediate prospect of leaving it, and returning to the dust, how consolatory is the first and great promise of the gospel of a resurrection to eternal life! The faithful follower of Christ, regarding *his* resurrection from the dead as a confirmation of this promise, believes that he has abolished death, and brought " life and immortality to light." And this faith becomes an anchor to his soul both sure and stedfast, which preserves him from sinking amidst the stormy billows of adversity, and assures him that he shall ere long reach the peaceful

ful shores of that everlasting inheritance which is reserved for him in heaven!

Such, my Christian brethren, is the treasure of truth, of wisdom, and of consolation, contained in the gospel. At the same time, think ye not that the man who first discovered this treasure, who first found this pearl of great price, acted wisely, in selling all that he had to purchase it? You admire the integrity, zeal, and fortitude, of the first apostles and disciples of Christ, and of the whole body of Christians in the early ages of the church, who, in the midst of severe trials and cruel persecutions, boldly embraced, and stedfastly adhered to, the Christian faith—who through much tribulation entered into the kingdom of heaven—let me ask you, do you not also admire their wisdom? Had they, who during our Saviour's life enjoyed the benefit of his instructions and example, and who by his death and resurrection were confirmed in the belief of all the great truths which

he

in favour of equity and humanity, it provides for the removal of every occasion of offence and confusion, and lays a sure foundation for public as well as private tranquillity. After this brief survey of the general spirit and leading features of the Christian law, may I not with confidence appeal to your best judgment to determine, whether the gospel is not a rich treasury of moral wisdom?

I add, thirdly, our holy religion furnishes us with inestimable treasures of divine consolation.

In the hour of affliction, when the heart is overwhelmed with trouble, Christianity directs us to sources of comfort more substantial and satisfying than any which philosophy can boast. Instead of absurdly requiring us to call in question the testimony of our senses, and to think that to be no pain which we feel to be such; instead of leaving us under the iron yoke of blind fatality, and instructing us that it is in vain to be afflicted at evils

which

which we cannot avoid, when that very circumstance is in reality the most just ground of affliction; instead of leaving us, at seasons when we most need consolation, without any other relief than vain speculations and unnatural exertions, Christianity directs our faith to a wise and gracious Providence; by which all events, however afflictive, are rendered, in the issue, productive of benefit: it presents before us an animating pattern of patience in Jesus, " the author and finisher of our faith," whom the genuine principles and spirit of religion enabled, in the immediate prospect of crucifixion, to say— " Not my will, but thine be done." In fine, it directs our views and hopes towards a future life, where our present light afflictions, if patiently endured and wisely improved, will work out for us a far more exceeding and eternal weight of glory.

Under the consciousness of guilt, when the wounded spirit looks, with trembling apprehension, towards that righteous Judge, he had taught them concerning God and religion, concerning the forgiveness of sins and everlasting life—had these men, as soon as they found that their adherence to the cause of Christ would subject them to obloquy, and even to worldly losses and bodily sufferings, determined to abandon so unprofitable and hazardous a profession, and with it to resign all the spiritual blessings and heavenly hopes of the gospel; instead of resolutely executing their commission, and, in the face of hardships and hazards, going from city to city, and from country to country, propagating this new religion, had the apostles quietly returned to their respective occupations, and made the best of their lot in this world, without paying any farther regard to what their Master had taught them concerning another, would not their conduct have been, not merely pusillanimous, but foolish. Convinced as they were of the Divine authority of their great Leader, and of the truth of the promise of eternal life,

which

which through the whole course of his ministry he had taught them to regard as the grand message which he was appointed to deliver to them from the Father; to have deserted the post assigned them, as soon as they found it becoming hazardous, would have been preferring momentary safety and temporary possessions to immortal glory and an everlasting inheritance; it would have been relinquishing heaven for earth.

If the first Christians, surrounded as they were with difficulties and terrors, would have acted unwisely, had they not parted with all that they had, to secure the possession of the treasures of the gospel which they had found:—Reflect, my fellow Christians, in what light your conduct must appear, in the eye of impartial reason, if, having this precious treasure in your hands, you neglect to use it for the purposes for which it is bestowed. Through the bounty of Divine Providence, it is your happy lot to enjoy the peaceful

peaceful possession of that treasure, which at the first acquisition cost the lives of many excellent men. You find yourselves as securely invested with this treasure, by inheritance from your parents, as with any other patrimony: and so far are you from being obliged to defend it at the hazard of every thing dear and valuable to you in this world, that you could not relinquish it, at least your *nominal* property in it, without some discredit. Your Christian faith, as far as respects the mere profession, costs you nothing. How inexcusable, then, must you be, if you suffer so rich a gift, so freely bestowed, to lie by you unemployed!

The Christian religion, be it remembered, like every other treasure, in order to be profitable, must be used. As gold and silver are of no value to their possessor whilst they remain locked up in his coffers; so the truths, the precepts, and the promises, of the gospel, can make no man wiser,

wiser, better, or more happy, whilst, through ignorance or inattention, they lie by neglected: *the New Testament, with respect to him, remains a sealed book.* It is only by studying the doctrine of Christ till you understand its meaning, that you can be qualified to derive any benefit from Christianity. It is only by establishing in your minds the principles of religion and morality which Christ hath taught; by applying his precepts and examples to yourselves in the actual conduct of life; and by frequently contemplating his promises with an immediate view to your own condition and prospects, that you can in reality become possessed of those blessings which Christianity offers you, religious knowledge, moral wisdom, peaceful reflections, and heavenly hopes. These are the ultimate treasures towards which, as Christians, you are taught to aspire. Christianity itself is a treasure only as it conducts men to the possession of these: and though you are already, without any cost or pains, in possession of the former, you will not be able to possess yourselves of the latter without some labour and expence. If you wish to acquire the knowledge and wisdom which Christianity places within your reach, you must redeem some portion of your time from business or pleasure, for reflecting upon the important subjects to which the gospel directs your thoughts. If you be desirous of obtaining the consolations of religion under all the vicissitudes of the present life, and of entitling yourselves to that everlasting inheritance which Christ hath set before you, you must purchase your title to it at the expence of all your vicious pleasures and all your unrighteous gains. You must part with every criminal passion, though it be dear to you as a right hand or a right eye. You must resign all your prospects of enriching yourselves by fraud or oppression. You must be willing, if not to sell all that you have and give to the poor (a condition which the present

state

state of society does not require), yet to minister freely of your abundance to the necessities of your brethren, in hopes that having sowed bountifully, you shall hereafter reap also bountifully.

Be exhorted, then, my Christian brethren, to regard the treasure of the gospel as a talent entrusted to you by the great Lord of all, for which you must hereafter give an account; and remember, that if, through negligence or perverseness, you hide your Lord's talent in the earth, you will inevitably expose yourselves to the condemnation of the *wicked and slothful servant*.

" We Christians," says the excellent Archbishop Tillotson, " have certainly the best and holiest, the wisest, and most reasonable religion in the world; but then we are in the worst condition of all mankind, if the best religion in the world do not make us good."

On the moral Abuse of Words.

ISAIAH v. 20.

Woe unto them that call evil good, and good evil.

The sentiment which the prophet intended to convey by these words was probably this, that the most fatal consequences are to be apprehended from that moral depravity which confounds men's ideas of right and wrong, and leads them to regard that conduct as innocent and meritorious, which is in fact base and criminal: and this is, doubtless, an important practical doctrine, which might profitably employ our present meditations. But I have made choice of the words, in order to direct your attention to a topic, which,

which, though of a more limited nature, may perhaps be found productive of much seasonable and useful instruction. The topic I mean is, the mischievous effects of the propensity, so common among mankind, to affix false names to moral qualities and characters—to gloss over culpable dispositions, and bad actions, by giving them a soft appellation—and, on the contrary, to depreciate real excellence, by annexing to it some degrading term, thus " calling evil, good; and good, evil."

It has long been well understood, that accuracy in the use of words is of fundamental importance in writing: but it has not, perhaps, been equally attended to, that the same kind of accuracy is equally necessary, both in the cultivation of the understanding, and in the conduct of life. With respect to the former, I might easily prove to you, by a variety of instances, that a great part of the disputes which are carried on with so much acrimony, whether on political, moral, or religious subjects, are owing either to a careless misapprehension, or a wilful misinterpretation of the meaning of words; and that, in order to bring many controversies to an amicable termination, little more would be necessary, than to prevail upon the disputants to settle with precision the signification of the leading terms which they employ, and always to use them, on both sides, exactly in the same sense. But, waving this view of the subject, I shall confine myself in this discourse to the consideration of the unhappy influence of the inaccurate use, or the designed perversion and abuse, of words, upon moral conduct: and I shall find no difficulty in collecting examples of this perversion and abuse from real life, abundantly sufficient to convince you of the necessity of being continually upon your guard, lest you be perverted in sentiment, and misled in conduct, by the common practice of calling evil good, and good evil.

I shall

I shall first enumerate several instances in which men give fair names to foul actions, or call evil good; remarking, as we proceed, the mischievous consequences arising from this abuse of words.

At the head of the list, no one instance of this moral perversion of language can be more properly placed than that which disgraces almost every page of the history of religion, calling *intolerance* and *persecution, zeal for the cause of God.* To restrain men by violent means from the free exercise of their rational powers on subjects of infinite moment to each individual, must have, at first sight, appeared such a flagrant act of injustice—to check the unreserved communication of ideas on questions, on which it must be for the general benefit that knowledge should be as far as possible extended, must have been so evidently inconsistent with political wisdom—to subject conscientious inquirers after truth, and sincere professors of religion, to grievous pains and
penalties

penalties for actions in their nature highly meritorious, could not but have been thought such a gross violation of equity and humanity—that, while civil or ecclesiastical rulers viewed this treatment of their fellow-creatures in its full deformity, under its proper appellation, persecution, it is scarcely to be conceived that they should have been able to reconcile themselves to so heinous an enormity. From the naked character of a persecutor, the heart of man would revolt with horror. But change the term by which this violent stretch of power is described—instead of persecution, call it zeal for the glory of God, and for the purity of the Christian faith, and immediately it assumes a new aspect: the folly, the injustice, the inhumanity of the proceeding, instantly vanish; the feelings of nature are on a sudden benumbed; the honest struggles of conscience are suppressed; and the persecutor, instead of reproaching himself for barbarity, ranks himself with pride among

among the faithful servants of God. In this manner it was that Persecution, with all her unnatural horrors, supported herself through long ages of darkness; and by this artifice she has been able, even in the midst of the light of reformation, to postpone to a distant period the moment in which, by the universal suffrage of mankind, she should be consigned to eternal infamy.

Turn your attention, next, to that most unnatural and shocking state of human society, *war*, and you will find that a misapplication and abuse of terms has, in no small degree, contributed to cast a delusive lustre over its horrors and enormities. War, when it is strictly and properly *defensive*, that is, when it is undertaken merely for the protection of life, liberty, and property, against unprovoked and outrageous assault, may be vindicated on the first principle of human nature, self-preservation. Even in this case, however, far from being contemplated with admiration,

admiration, it ought to be deprecated, as only not the greatest evil incident to society. But, in whatever case war is *offensive*, or is voluntarily undertaken for the sake of conquest, or from any other motive of ambition or avarice; on account of the numerous calamities which it brings upon mankind, it can deserve to be regarded with no other feelings than those of horror and indignation. A war of conquest is, in truth, nothing better than a plan of plunder, devastation, and slaughter; not the less, but the more to be dreaded and abhorred for the systematic regularity with which it is conducted, and for the " pomp and circumstance" which surround it. Had the Alexanders and Cæsars, whose ambition has, in successive ages, deluged the earth with blood, been known by no other appellations than those to which their military achievements entitled them, their names would have been transmitted to posterity with infamy, as foremost in the list of robbers

robbers and murderers. But no sooner is the robber and the murderer, by the magic of words, converted into a hero, and his destructive ravages into glorious exploits, than the criminality of the character is lost in its splendour; and while we admire the prowess of the warrior, we forget the injustice and cruelty of the man.

A similar delusion arises from the abuse of words in private quarrels. Let the fashionable method of deciding disputes by duelling—a practice which originated in a barbarous age, and is a disgrace to an enlightened and civilized nation—be allowed to wear its proper name; and there are few persons so totally destitute of religious and moral principle, that they would not shrink from it with horror. Whether the motive which immediately urges men to the practice be violent resentment and a thirst of revenge, or whether, as is perhaps more commonly the case, it be a slavish respect to arbitrary notions

tions of honour, and a desire of preventing or wiping off a suspicion of cowardice; the action itself, necessarily implying a deliberate intention to take away the life of another, in a manner not authorized either by the laws of God or man, in the judgment of reason can merit no milder appellation than murder: and the circumstance of the duellist's exposing his own life, instead of diminishing, aggravates the guilt; for wantonly to hazard life, is at once an act of injustice to society, and of impiety towards God. Thus the point would unquestionably be determined in the court of conscience. But bring this offence before another court, instituted by caprice, and sanctioned by custom, where the law of honour supplies the place of the law of reason, and what was before a murderous deed is now only *an affair of honour*; and under that appellation, not only ceases to be thought criminal or shameful, but becomes a subject of applause.

But

But this is, by no means, the only instance of the pernicious folly I am describing which is to be met with in that class of mankind which distinguishes itself by the name of the polite world. Among the giddy votaries of fashion and pleasure, how frequently do we meet with instances of young people, who, in consequence of this absurd misapplication of terms, are admired and applauded for those very things for which they merit contempt and censure! A youth, for example, who merely from the want of sufficient vigour of intellect, or through a culpable habit of indolence, has never formed any steady principles or regular plan of life, and who, only because he has no judgment or will of his own, gives himself up to the humours or passions of others, shall obtain praise for that pliableness of disposition and unsteadiness of character, which at best can only deserve to be pitied as a weakness, and which may probably betray him into vice and ruin:
whilst

whilst another, who is endued by nature with a more strong and active mind, but whose impetuous ardour has not been duly restrained by discipline, or regulated by precept, shall be spoken of with applause for daring to overleap the boundaries of decorum, and to trample under foot the established laws of order. Thus do *thoughtless folly* and *wild excess* assume the names and bear away the honours of *good-nature* and *manly spirit*. What mischievous confusion arises from the same cause in men's ideas of the virtues of moderation, sobriety, and chastity! Let the *vain* and *ambitious* man indulge his ruling propensity to what excess he may—let him lavish his patrimony with the most thoughtless profusion in articles of luxury and splendour—let him, in order to support his extensive mode of living, draw with the boldest hand upon the property of others—let the frugal and industrious tradesman, and even the needy mechanic and labourer, by means of an unreasonable demand

demand of credit, or by other acts of extortion and oppreſſion, be compelled to ſend in their hard-earned contributions towards furniſhing the ſuperfluities of his table, the elegancies of his manſion, and the magnificence of his retinue; all this may paſs without cenſure, may obtain applauſe, as long as he can perſuade the world to call his fooliſh and ruinous *prodigality* by the captivating name of *hoſpitality* or *generoſity*. While the *intemperate* man is daily indulging his appetite without reſtraint, and yielding to the ſtrong impulſe of an habit of inebriety, in a degree, which, whether attended with actual intoxication or not, muſt inevitably impair his faculties, and undermine his conſtitution; how does he find means to perſuade himſelf, that he is doing nothing more than innocently enjoying the gifts of nature? Strangely perverting the meaning of words, he conceals from himſelf the folly and criminality of his conduct, by calling his

drunkenneſs

drunkenness and *gluttony good-living*.—
The violation of *chastity* is a crime so
injurious to society, and productive of so
much personal and domestic infelicity,
that it becomes necessary for those who
addict themselves to it, to hide its turpi-
tude from their sight, by forgetting, as
much as possible, those appellations with
which no other ideas are associated than
those of sinfulness and guilt, and by assuming in their stead such terms as rather
convey the idea of pleasure than of criminality. And, whether it be that even
the virtuous part of the world is inclined
to shew so much lenity to vices of this
class, or whether it is to be wholly ascribed to false delicacy, certain it is that
licentiousness meets with too much con-
nivance, and even countenance, from the
soft appellations under which it commonly passes. *Gallantry* is a term which
may be mentioned without calling up a
blush upon the cheek of modesty; and a

gay young man is a character which virtue itself, perhaps, sometimes contemplates almost without a frown. But it ought never to be forgotten by those who have any concern for the preservation of good morals, that these and other apparently innocent appellations are in reality expressive of heinous and destructive vices; and that, with whatever lenity men may be inclined, in the present relaxed state of manners, to treat offenders of this class, "Whoremongers and adulterers God will judge."

It were easy to extend this enumeration of instances, in which men "call evil good," much further. I might, for example, direct your attention to the crafty knave, who while he is guilty of direct violations of honesty, endeavours to silence his conscience by calling the fraudulent practices, by which he is daily enriching himself, *mysteries of trade*; to the sordid slave of avarice, who thinks he
sufficiently

sufficiently justifies his conduct in turning a deaf ear to every solicitation of humanity, by giving his *covetousness* the name of *prudent economy*; to the malicious slanderer, who strives to throw a lustre even upon the blackness of calumny, by calling it *satirical wit*; or, lastly, to the profane scoffer at religion, who offers an insult to reason by calling his *daring impiety, philosophical freedom*. But I pass over these, in order to leave time for illustrating by a few examples the contrary fault, equally common, and scarcely less pernicious, of bringing amiable and excellent qualities and characters into discredit, by giving them unworthy and degrading appellations, or " calling good evil."

Evident as it is that the principles of religion will bear the test of the most diligent and rigorous examination; natural as it is to the heart of man to cherish sentiments of reverence and gratitude towards

wards the great Author of nature; delightful and beneficial as religious exercises have been found in fact to be, by those who have cultivated a spirit of devotion, how frequently has it been seen that young persons have been discouraged from the public avowal of religious principles, and from the regular practice of religious duties, by the mere force of that ridicule which consists in nothing else but boldly affixing a name of contempt to a thing entitled to every epithet expressive of value and dignity! What injury has been done to the cause of religion; what unmerited reproach has been brought upon its professors, by the injudicious use of the terms *enthusiasm* and *fanaticism*, or by the indiscriminate and contemptuous application of the character of *canting hypocrite!* Men choose rather to be thought to have no religion, than to be laughed at as fools, or despised as knaves.

The right of private judgment is one

of the sacred and unalienable rights of man. To inquire after truth with an honest and unprejudiced mind, is a duty of universal obligation. One of the most meritorious services which any one can render to his species is, to endeavour to dissipate the clouds of error, and diffuse the light of truth, by freely communicating the result of diligent inquiry and close reflection on subjects interesting to humanity. But who will find sufficient inducement to pass through the necessary labour of research and study, when, if his inquiries should happen to lead him out of the track of popular opinion, he can have no other alternative, than either to bury the result in his own bosom, or to expose himself to unmerited odium under the appellation of an *Innovator?* Or what degree of public spirit will be powerful enough to incite the most able and succesful inquirer to undertake the benevolent task of enlightening the world, when his new opinions, merely because they

they are such, though certainly entitled to a candid examination, will be instantly stamped with the opprobrious character of *heresy*; and when the least injurious return he can possibly expect from society is, to have that appellation, which ought to be conferred upon him as a title of honour, cast in his teeth as a term of reproach, and instead of being admired, to be stigmatised as a *philosopher?*

If we step into the moral walks of life, shall we not continually hear, and that too from persons who would by no means be thought to have cast off all reverence for virtue—a kind of language which, instead of supporting and encouraging virtue, can scarcely fail to put it out of countenance?—Is any one punctiliously exact in his adherence to the rules of equity, refraining with the utmost caution, not only from such encroachments upon the property of another as are subject to legal animadversion, but from all those smaller trespasses which can only

be felt by a mind deeply imbued with a delicate sense of honour, and well instructed to distinguish between good and evil? his *unalloyed honesty*, which entitles him to distinguished respect as the possessor of a rare jewel, among the bold adventurers in search of gain, will hardly escape the sneer of contempt under the name of *weak scrupulosity*. Does any one possess in an uncommon degree, that sweetness of temper and gentleness of spirit, which will render him tranquil under affronts, and patient under injuries; or has he, by diligently cultivating Christian meekness, acquired that degree of moral strength and elevation of mind, which enable him to practise the sublime virtue of forgiveness; with those who bring every character to the arbitrary standard of false honour, his superior merit is in a moment annihilated, by branding it with the infamous appellations of *pusillanimity* and *cowardice*.—To redeem the honour of human nature, does an exalted character
sometimes

sometimes arise, like a new star in the heavens, and surprise the world by exhibiting a bright example of pure, disinterested, and active benevolence? In the execution of some noble design, for the relief of misery, the correction of error, or the diffusion of knowledge, virtue and happiness, does this generous friend and benefactor of his kind forego every consideration of personal indulgence and private interest, pass through a long course of labour and fatigue, expend his wealth, and even expose his life to hazard, and his good name to obloquy?—even this subblimity of virtue, which may be conceived in some sort to assimilate the human nature to the Divine, when judged of by minds too little to comprehend its grandeur, or too base to revere what they despair of imitating, is pitied as a weakness or condemned as a crime. The *humane Howard* was called a *fanatic*: the *wise* Socrates was condemned as a *corrupter of youth*: even the benevolent *Jesus,*

Jesus, that Divine teacher, whose doctrine breathed no other spirit than piety towards God, and good-will towards men, was reproached as a *blasphemer* of God, and a *perverter of the people*.

Thus generally prevalent is that moral abuse of words which consists in calling evil good, and good evil. How mischievous it is in its effects, must have in part appeared from the preceding detail, and will be still further evident to every one who reflects upon the fascinating power of words on the imagination and passions. Confer upon *vice* the name of *pleasure*, its deformity, its criminality, its fatal consequences, will disappear; and it will come before the mind associated with all that is captivating and delightful. On the contrary, let virtue in general, or any of its branches, be denominated by terms expressive of labour and mortification, or adapted to excite contempt or aversion, the ideas and feelings commonly associated with these terms are most injuriously

ously transferred to the qualities and characters to which the terms are applied. By this artifice men are continually deceiving themselves, and imposing upon others; bestowing upon bad characters the praise which is due only to the good; and bringing ridicule and disgrace upon characters which are entitled to respect and esteem. What difficulties and discouragements are hereby cast in the way of the well-disposed; what protection and countenance is given to absurd follies and destructive vices, may be easily conceived. Much, then, does it concern every one, who wishes either to preserve in his own mind a just abhorrence of vice and a becoming reverence for virtue, or to check the encroachments of the one, and promote the interests of the other, in the world around him, to avoid the pernicious practice of calling evil good, and good evil.—Scarcely less have those good men to answer for, who, through culpable timidity or false politeness, bestow soft

and

and palliating appellations upon heinous immoralities, than those bad men, who, in order to screen their own vices, are continually endeavouring to bring the strict and conscientious practice of virtue into discredit by loading it with opprobrious names.

The true and only remedy for this great and growing evil is, to pay more regard to things than to words; and to impress upon the mind a strong and habitual conviction, that independently of the caprice of language, and the tyranny of fashion, the nature of things must for ever remain unalterably the same; that good will still *be* good, and evil will still *be* evil, by whatever names they may be called; and that as long as human nature shall exist, virtue will continue to be wisdom and happiness, and vice to be folly and misery

Against thinking ill of the World.

Psalm cxvi. 11.

I said in my haste, All men are liars.

A PRUDENT man will always decide upon characters with caution. A benevolent man will not censure at random, or admit an opinion injurious to the reputation of another without reluctance. "Charity hopeth all things."

It was in an evil and unguarded hour that the unlimited censure of the text was uttered. The Psalmist had been greatly afflicted. Perhaps he had recently felt some of those injuries of which he so pathetically complains in other psalms. Perhaps his sensibility had been wounded,

wounded, not by open hostility from an avowed enemy, from whom he could have expected no kindness, but from the secret treachery of some false friend, in whom he had implicitly and affectionately confided. Unable to endure the pain of such a wound, he sought relief from his vexation, not in particular resentment against the person who had injured him, but in a general invective against mankind; he charged the whole species with the base depravity and criminality of a wilful and deliberate violation of truth; he said, "All men are liars."

David seems to have been sensible of the injustice of his censure, for he ascribes it to that precipitate judgment which is the effect of passion: "I said *in my haste*, all men are liars;" herein expressing disapprobation of the assertion, and a wish to retract it. Supposing him to have done so, let us not, then, set down the uncharitable censure as an indelible blot upon his character; especially as it was uttered

uttered in a moment of perturbation, when he was greatly afflicted.

In some such evil moment many an one has been tempted, like the Psalmist, to extend his unfavourable opinion of an individual to mankind in general, and with misanthropic spleen to wish that they could retire from the haunts of men into some peaceful retreat, where they should no longer be disturbed by human follies and vices. Nor are these general censures of the human species confined merely to those from whom disappointment and vexation have called forth such hasty exclamations as that of the text. From various causes, there are not a few whose deliberate judgment in a great measure coincides with the rash censure, uttered in a moment of ill humour, by the Psalmist. Some religious persons entertain such humiliating notions of the depravity and corruption of human nature, and are disposed to understand with such literal rigour those expressions in the Scriptures

Scriptures which describe the degeneracy of mankind, that they believe the whole human race to be, in their natural disposition, prone to wickedness, and do not even except themselves from this grievous reproach. Others, from a system of opinions which rejects all idea of Divine Providence and a moral government of the world, have deduced conclusions equally unfavourable. Finding, as they have imagined, nothing but disorder and confusion in the moral world, they have inferred that there is no provision in the constitution of human nature for the establishment of virtuous principles, and that men are left by nature to the casual direction of caprice or passion. Without entering into any abstract speculations, others draw similar inferences from a few unfavourable facts which have happened to fall in their way. Having been led by personal misfortunes to entertain gloomy notions of human life, and having, withal, suffered repeated inconveniencies niences and injuries from the treachery and unkindness of persons concerning whom they once entertained a favourable opinion, they not only at first pronounce, in their haste, a severe censure on mankind, but admit a deliberate and settled opinion, that no such thing as disinterested generosity, or sterling honesty is to be found in the world. Or, lastly, having in the course of an extensive acquaintance with the world, been witness to much craft and chicanery, much meanness and duplicity, and innumerable examples of downright fraud and knavery; perhaps, too, having in some degree caught the infection of the manners of which they have been spectators, and contracted some portion of that illiberality of sentiment, and obliquity of character, of which they complain, have embraced, and maintained it as their settled opinion, that the appearances of virtue, which attract so much admiration from the young and unexperienced, are almost universally nothing better than the pretensions of hypocrisy to answer some selfish and sinister purpose; and, in short, that it is in vain to search on earth for that, so much boasted, noblest work of God, an honest man.

These severe censures upon mankind, produced from such various causes, and pronounced with such different views, facts will oblige us to confess, are not altogether without foundation. It is too manifest to be disputed, that in every period of the world, and every stage of civilization, the catalogue of human vices has been large. However mortifying the concession, it must be admitted, that even in the present enlightened age the progress of morality has not kept pace with the advancement of knowledge, and that society still abounds with depraved and vicious characters, which are a disgrace to our common nature. Nevertheless, we are not authorised from these appearances to draw a general conclusion against

against human nature, and to say that "all men are wicked."

For let it, in the first place, be considered, that no individual is sufficiently acquainted with the characters of others, to draw a general conclusion of this kind from the facts which come before him. It is but little that any one can know of the characters of men, I will not say in the world at large, but even in the place in which he resides. We are often imposed upon by deceitful appearances, even concerning those with whom we are most intimately conversant; and we are at all times very imperfectly acquainted with the principles and motives which influence men's actions, without an accurate knowledge of which it is impossible to form a true estimate of any character. Add to this, that few persons are sufficiently free from the bias of passion, sufficiently attentive to the varieties of characters which are presented before them, or sufficiently deliberate and cautious in judging of individual characters, to be qualified to pronounce a decisive sentence against the human race.

The observations, however, which every man makes, and must necessarily make, upon the characters of others, are sufficient to justify him in concluding that human society is composed of good and bad men, as the same field produces both wheat and tares. Let any take a candid survey of that portion of human society which lies within the sphere of his own observation, and he must be very unfortunate indeed in his situation, if he do not find a sufficient number of good and worthy characters to rescue human nature from the reproach of universal depravity. If we sometimes meet with men who openly avow their dereliction of every principle of religion, and every moral obligation, and have the effrontery to confess that they know only one rule of conduct, that every man is to take care of himself without regarding what becomes

comes of others; such men are rare monsters in the moral world, seldom seen, and when met with, only gazed at with astonishment and horror. If in the present artificial, and in many respects corrupt, state of society, false notions of honour are embraced which militate against the first principles of religion and virtue—and which, in some instances, under the imperious and irresistible authority of custom, prompt men to commit, or, which in moral estimation is the same thing, to attempt to commit, crimes from which the feeling and virtuous mind revolts with horror—it is to be considered that these absurd and mischievous notions prevail only in a small part of the community, and affect that part only occasionally, and partially; and that the generality of mankind are still content to acknowledge, in all cases, the supreme authority of conscience and of God. In the transactions of commercial life, can it be doubted that men commonly observe the law of honesty, and that the violations of this law, which take place between the buyer and the seller, though frequent, are, after all, only occasional exceptions to a general rule? It is sometimes asserted, in proof of the general depravity of the world, that it is impossible, in the present state of things, that a man of business who is strictly honest should prosper; and that, therefore, every man who wishes to make his way in the world, must bend his conscience to his situation, and relax in some measure the ties of moral obligation, by which in a purer state of society he might be more strictly bound. Without retorting upon those who make such assertions the uncandid insinuation, that they judge of the general character of the world by their own, we may be allowed to ask, whether it would be possible for society to subsist at all upon the supposition, that fraud and falsehood were as common as truth and honesty are at present? What, in that case, would become of that mutual

tual confidence which is the foul of commercial intercourse? Would not the general failure of integrity produce universal distrust? and what could arise from universal distrust but universal confusion? Bad as the world is, it is, then, not true, nor approaching to the truth, that all men are knaves, or that all men are liars.

The fact on the present question is so clear, that the matter may be safely rested on an appeal to the most gloomy and discontented misanthrope, or to the most severe and rigid judge of human characters. Where is the man who will not acknowledge, that though he may have been disappointed in many of his reasonable expectations from others, his connexions with his fellow-creatures have afforded no proof that every man has been devising evil, and practising mischief against him? who, if he speak the truth, must honestly confess, that those around him have, on the whole, done him little injustice, and shewn him much kindness. No one, who is not abfolutely without friend or brother—who does not, in the midft of fociety, live as folitary and joylefs as the torpid monk in his cell—who is not continually oppreffed and wretched, through the injuftice and cruelty of his brethren—can have any pretence for paffing an unbounded cenfure on mankind.

With refpect to the generality of perfons in the ordinary fituations of life, I will be bold to affert, that their experience can afford them no plea for indulging fuch gloomy ideas of human life, or fuch fplenetic feelings towards their fpecies; and it deferves ferious confideration, that the indulgence of fuch ideas and fuch feelings is highly injurious.

One of the moft obvious effects of fuch an opinion of the world is, to produce or cherifh ill-temper. It can fcarcely be fuppofed, that this habit can be formed but in a mind already predifpofed to fevere and cenforious judgment by a temper naturally turned towards fpleen and fretfulnefs.

fretfulnefs. It might be fairly expected, that a mere error of the judgment on the general character of mankind would be, if not prevented, at leaft corrected, by the genial influence of habitual good-humour. The man whofe cheerful and eafy difpofition inclines him to be pleafed with every thing about him, will not readily admit opinions concerning the world which would tend to difturb his tranquillity, and deftroy his happinefs. But, however this be, it is very evident, that no man can long indulge unfavourable fentiments concerning mankind, without having his temper fretted and foured: for who, that has any right feelings left, can be happy, while he imagines himfelf living in the midft of a race of hypocrites and deceivers?

Another natural and unavoidable confequence of thinking ill of mankind in general, is a difpofition to fufpect the honefty and fincerity of individuals. A man who entertains fuch an opinion of his fpecies, muft must suppose the exceptions to the general character to be exceedingly rare, and will therefore with difficulty persuade himself that he has been so fortunate as to find many of these exceptions within the small circle of his own connexions. He will think it more probable, that the good opinion which he has been led to entertain of his friends, has been the effect of that partial affection which blinds the judgment. Hence, when the first impulses of kindness or good-nature would prompt him to think well of another, his pernicious system checks the generous emotions of his heart, and he judges it reasonable to suspect that he is mistaken. Jealousies, fears, and alarms, rise up in every quarter. Questioning every man's honesty, he will scarcely venture to credit any man's word. Some unfriendly thought, some sinister design, he will see lurking under every smile; and in every friend he will apprehend a deceiver, in every brother a supplanter.

"With

"With ill-temper and suspicion will naturally be united censoriousness. Though he who believes that " all men are liars," must think that there is a good deal of false accusation and calumny in the world, and might be supposed the less inclined to listen to the lying tongue of slander; yet, at the same time, believing as he does that the generality of mankind are bad, he will judge it probable, independent of the authority of testimony, that, in any given instance, an evil report is better entitled to credit than a good one. While, therefore, he is deaf to the praises which singular merit sometimes extorts from reluctant lips, he with a greedy ear devours up the overflowings of other people's ill-nature and pride. With respect to himself, he has no restraint upon the rigour of his strictures and the severity of his censures upon the character and conduct of his neighbours; for, according to his settled opinion of human nature, the more rigorous and severe, the more likely are they

they to accord with the real fact. To be candid is, in his judgment, to be weak; to think men good, till you have some positive proof that they are otherwise, he conceives to be shutting your eyes in a path beset with snares, till your feet are entangled. In a bad world like this, he deems it wisest and safest, in our judgments of characters, to lean to the side of censoriousness; and he ridicules and despises that charity which " believeth all things."

The natural result of all this must be an unsocial and churlish disposition. A bad opinion of mankind must impair the social principle, and weaken the social affections. The general notion of the dishonesty and depravity of mankind will not float at large upon the surface of society, without attaching itself to individuals, and bringing every one, in some degree, under the influence of dark suspicion; whence must necessarily arise a strong propensity to peevishness and ill-humour,

humour, which will at length settle its muddy waters into the stagnant pool of misanthropy. If the countenance is brightened and the heart cheered by the sight of those whom we esteem; if, as Solomon says truly, " iron sharpeneth iron, so a man sharpeneth the countenance of his friend," it must be true, on the contrary, that daily intercourse with persons whom we have taught ourselves to suspect or to despise, must be a perpetual source of dissatisfaction and disgust. With such ideas and feelings, it is impossible that the heart should expand itself in the generous sympathies of social life, or yield itself up to the free enjoyment of its pleasures. To the mind thus enveloped with the mist of uncharitableness, the world will present no gay and cheering prospects; solitude will appear preferable to society; and nothing will remain but to prefer the dreary wilderness to the crowded city; or, perhaps, to think life a burden, and to adopt, as the deliberate

language

language of settled spleen, the exclamation which was uttered by Job under the strong pressure of accumulated afflictions, " I loath it; I would not live always."

The splenetic misanthrope must be discontented. All nature wears to him the dark hue of his own gloomy ideas. For want of worthy objects on which to exercise his benevolent and social feelings, his mind must unavoidably prey upon itself. Disappointed in all the delightful expectations from the world, which in happier moments of honest confidence and eager hope he had entertained, and not perceiving that the fault is not so much in the world as in himself, he rashly and peevishly concludes that there is nothing in life worth living for, and drags on a heavy and restless existence full of disquietude and vexation.

It will be well if such notions and such feelings do not finally terminate in diliberate dissatisfaction with the present order of nature, and in impious complaints and

and censures of the ways of Providence: for upon what principle can the man, who thinks the generality of mankind wicked and wretched, assure himself that they are under the government of a wise and good Being, who intends them to be virtuous and happy? Believing that mankind are universally corrupt in principle and vicious in practice, he must conclude it to be the design of the Almighty Ruler that it should be so; and will not, therefore, easily discern, in the present constitution of the world, proofs of a wise and righteous moral government, or indications of a gradual correction and melioration, which will finally issue in universal happiness; the consummation which every benevolent heart must devoutly wish, and towards which every one, who views the world with a candid and enlightened mind, may look with confident expectation.

A settled disposition to think ill of mankind is, then, not a mere error of judgment, or idle fancy, which may be innocently

cently and safely indulged: it is an unjust and malignant censure upon a whole race of fellow-creatures contradictory to fact and experience: it is a perverse humour, productive in the mind which indulges it of uneasy and restless passions, and tending, in the general state of society, to overturn the grand pillars of human happiness, social confidence, and religious hope. It is therefore the interest of every man to guard the avenues of his mind with the utmost vigilance against the intrusion of this troublesome and dangerous guest. Though we may be disposed to excuse, in ourselves or others, those casual ebullitions of spleen and uncharitableness which arise from some temporary cause of vexation—from the inconstancy and treachery, for example, of a friend, on whom we have bestowed affectionate esteem and unlimited confidence, we should industriously and resolutely avoid every approach towards a habit of general and indiscriminate censure. Harsh reflections,

flections, and even unkind thoughts of individuals, are blameable, not only on account of the immediate injustice which they imply, but on account of their baneful influence on the judgment we form of our species. Speculative systems, which have a tendency to generate misanthropy, should be carefully examined before they are embraced; for it is not very probable that any tenet is true which would lead men to hate one another. In fine, every thing in human nature and human life is capable of being viewed under two aspects, the bright and the gloomy; and it is our wisdom always to prefer the former to the latter. To think as well of one another and of all mankind as we fairly and honestly can, is prudent for ourselves, is equitable to our brethren, and is an act of piety to the great Author of our being.

Inattention to the Concerns of others reproved.

GENESIS iv. 9.

Am I my brother's keeper?

THESE were the words of the first murderer; and the language, or at least the sentiment, has been adopted by every villain and knave, by every tyrant and oppressor, by every churlish and selfish spirit, from the beginning of the world to this day.

When the haughty despot issues forth his mandates to bend the will of a whole empire to the will of one man, and makes his own ambition, resentment, or caprice, the only measures of his tyranny; what is

is the language of such conduct but this—
" The weak were made for the powerful; the many for the few; and millions, if by any means they can be brought under the dominion, ought to sacrifice their liberty, their property, their lives, to the will of one. Provided I am gratified, what is it to me, though thousands starve to supply my demands, though thousands fall to swell my ambition, or satiate my revenge?"

When the bold adventurer in search of gain explores far distant regions, with a cool and determined resolution, at all events, and at any price, to amass riches; when leaving behind him those troublesome attendants, honesty and humanity, he engages in enterprizes which must necessarily introduce poverty and wretchedness, perhaps famine and death, into the land of plenty; or when the restless son of avarice, neglecting the numerous means of acquiring wealth which an honest and liberal commerce affords, as too unproductive for his greedy thirst of gain, engages in plans of trade which are inconsistent with every principle of justice, or hostile to every feeling of humanity; when we see men, in this iniquitous manner, " making haste to be rich," what construction can candour itself put upon their conduct, but that their ruling passion is avarice, their first principle selfishness? If we were permitted to penetrate into their bosoms, what sentiments could we expect to find there but such as these?—" Wealth, the source of all pleasure and of all distinction, I see to be the only object worthy the attention of a wise man; and wealth, at all events, I am determined to gain. If it could be procured as expeditiously without wronging or injuring any one, I would neither be unjust nor oppressive: but schemes of trade that promise great profits must not be declined through squeamish delicacy.

I must

I muſt—no matter how—become rich and great."

Every one who has not ſhared the gains of iniquity, extortion, and cruelty, will eaſily perceive that ſuch methods of acquiring riches are inconſiſtent with every feeling of generoſity; and will find no difficulty in conceiving, that the thoughts and ſentiments which lead to ſuch actions are properly and emphatically expreſſed in the words of the text—" Am I my brother's keeper?" It may not, however, be equally eaſy to trace the features of ſelfiſhneſs, and develope its ſecret conceptions, in caſes in which our own intereſt is immediately concerned; and yet it is very certain, that inattention to the intereſts, and indifference to the welfare of others, is at the bottom of every fraudulent, injurious, or unkind action.

Is any man, for example, capable of adopting into his plan of buſineſs, however lawful and honourable in its general principle, any expedients by which he imposes upon the ignorance, or abuses the confidence, of those with whom he deals, diminishes the value of his goods, and clandestinely secures to himself exorbitant profits? Does any one, by false pretences of any kind, obtain from the world a degree of confidence and credit to which he is conscious he is not entitled, and hereby exposes others to losses and disappointments for the purpose of aggrandising himself? Are there any who, that they may gratify their own sportive or malignant humour, make no scruple of inventing tales injurious to the reputation of their neighbours, or circulating and magnifying, without any certain evidence, reports to their disadvantage? Is it the practice of any one to harass and oppress his dependants, by imposing upon them unreasonable burdens, or by withholding from them those returns which may equitably be expected, or to disturb the peace of the families with

with which he is connected, and deftroy the happinefs of his relations and friends, by perpetually giving way to a peevifh, fplenetic, or paffionate temper? Laftly, is any one fo much a flave to his animal appetites and felfifh paffions as to gratify them at the expence of the peace, the property, or the innocence, of another? In all thefe cafes, and in every other, in which men provide for their own indulgence by invading the rights of others, the language of the action is—" Let every man provide for his own happinefs as well as he is able : for my part, I know no other obligation, and have no other care, but to make myfelf happy by every means in my power. What though for my gratification the fair bloffom of innocence be blafted, and the venerable pile of domeftic happinefs be overturned? What though the daily comfort of a long train of connexions and dependants be interrupted by my wayward humours or ungoverned paffions? What though my neighbour's character fuffer, or his property be deftroyed, to afford me amufement, or to provide me with the means of enjoyment? All this concerns not me—"Am I my brother's keeper?"

Such we fhould find to be the real fentiments—could we read them—of every felfifh character: and fince men of this difpofition have only one object, that of taking care of themfelves, they doubtlefs value themfelves on the prudence and fteadinefs with which they profecute their defign. Neverthelefs, I do not defpair of proving—if not to their fatisfaction, at leaft to that of every impartial and difpaffionate inquirer after happinefs—that the felfifh plan of life is unreafonable and abfurd, and cannot poffibly attain the end at which it aims: I have no doubt of being able to fhew, that a felfifh fpirit is ftrongly marked with the characters of FOLLY, MEANNESS, INJUSTICE, and IMPIETY.

The

The FOLLY of seeking happiness from ourselves alone, without regarding the interests of others, may be evident to every one who is capable of perceiving, that it is folly to contend against the immutable laws of nature. Upon the established order of things in human life, upon the original constitution of human nature, it is written in characters which all may understand, "No man liveth to himself." Suppose one of those selfish mortals, who are inclined, on every sacrifice which they make of the interest of others to their own, to justify themselves by saying, "Am I my brother's keeper?" suppose such a man placed in that *insulated* state, which seems so consonant to the feelings of his contracted mind; having neither labour nor ingenuity at his command, to provide for his wants, or to minister to his pleasures; no companion to enliven his solitude, no friend to share his repast, or participate his pleasures or his pains: were his abode a paradise,

there

there can be no doubt that he would be wretched. The heart of man, after all that has been said in praise of solitude, naturally leans towards society, and whilst it has any kindness left, " wants some object to be kind to." Not only are we dependent upon our brethren for all those supplies which are necessary to the support and comfort of life, but we are endued by nature with social affections, which prompt us to " go out of ourselves" for enjoyment. It is not till the heart is debased and corrupted by some sordid or criminal passion, that it becomes insensible to the pleasures of friendship, and the " dear charities" of domestic life. A man without kind sentiments and a generous heart, is a more imperfect and mutilated being than one who is born blind, or has lost a limb. What folly then can be superior to that, of detaching ourselves in affection from those to whom nature has united us by the indissoluble bond of dependence, and, by indulging none but the selfish passions, voluntarily excluding ourselves from the richest part of the field of enjoyment which nature has opened before us?

That a selfish character is a *mean* and *despicable* one, will be questioned by none who are not themselves wholly incapable of noble conceptions or generous actions: and to appeal to such men as judges of what is becoming in character, would be no less absurd than to refer to a blind man the decision of a dispute concerning the merits of a picture. Who that hath eyes to see, and a heart to feel, can refrain from despising the man, who, like certain insects, shuts himself up within the shell of his own concerns, and never looks beyond the narrow inclosure, except when he is impelled by his wants or his desires? When one sees a numerous race of mortals, who seem born for no other purpose but to consume the fruits of the ground*,

---

* Nos numeri fruges consumere nati. Hor.

incapable of every care, and strangers to every pleasure, which does not terminate in themselves, were it not possible to contrast this contemptible group with the select band of generous spirits, who are capable of sympathizing in the sorrows and participating the joys of all around them, and who find their own highest gratification in communicating happiness to others, one might be tempted to blush for one's species, and be ashamed to wear the name of *man*. It is fortunate for these despicable characters, that the sense of shame and the social feelings generally decline together, and that they who are incapable of generous actions are also insensible of their value; else it would be impossible for them to support the humiliating comparison of their own insignificance and meanness with the dignity and lustre which surround the character of the generous and humane.

But it is not with meanness and folly alone

alone that the selfish are chargeable; they are likewise responsible for the complicated guilt of injustice and impiety.

If selfishness had no other effect than to destroy all inclination towards generous action, it might justly be considered as iniquitous; for though any specific act of liberality or kindness cannot be claimed, under the same notion of right, as a legal debt may be demanded, yet there is a general obligation by which every man is bound to consult the interests and promote the felicity of others. Nature has implanted in every human breast a principle of benevolence and feelings of humanity, which every one is conscious that he ought to obey: and every man receives so many benefits, and so much felicity, from the friendly attention, the faithful service, or the generous bounty, of others, that it would be disingenuous and ungrateful, on his part, to make them no returns of kindness and liberality.

liberality. The general law of " doing as we would be done unto" is particularly applicable to the duties of charity. If we naturally and reasonably expect that others should treat us with courtesy, and, when our condition requires it, with humanity, it is easy to perceive that others, in similar circumstances, have the same claim upon us. But it is not merely by restraining their beneficence that selfishness renders men unjust: many instances might be enumerated of direct and shameful violations of the first and most sacred rights of human nature, into which men are seduced for want of a due attention to the claims and respect for the interests of others. The man who makes his beloved self the center of all his wishes and pursuits, will not only want sufficient inducements to exert himself for the benefit of others, but will find himself irresistibly impelled by self-love to break through every barrier of honour, equity, and

and humanity, which obstructs his progress in the road to wealth and power. It is, perhaps, impossible for a selfish man not to be unjust.

And in being unjust he becomes, by necessary consequence, *impious*. In enduing the human mind with a capacity of discerning between right and wrong, a sense of justice, and a principle of benevolence, the Almighty hath written his law upon our hearts, and instructed us that what he requires from us is, " to do justly and love mercy." By placing us in relations which call for the continual exercise of social affections, and making us dependent on each other for the supports and conveniencies, and for most of the enjoyments of life, he hath, in the most expressive manner, declared it to be his will, that mankind, uniting in various relations, should form one common interest, and exert their collected strength to accumulate a common stock of happiness. The numerous pleasures and advantages

vantages, which at present flow from the reciprocal exercise of generous affections, and the continual exchange of good offices, together with the inconveniences and miseries which unavoidably attend a contrary temper and practice, may justly be regarded as divine sanctions for the reward of a benevolent, and the punishment of a selfish spirit. If to this we add, that it hath pleased the Eternal Father to send Jesus Christ, his beloved son, into the world, to deliver to mankind his express commandment, that they should love one another, and to assure them that the decisions of the final judgment, and the subsequent recompence, will be, in a great degree, regulated by the regard which has in this life been paid to the duties of beneficence; no doubt can remain, that the practice of the social and most acceptable virtues is an essential branch of religion, and that selfishness, with all the sordid and pernicious vices which attend in its train, is highly displeasing to God.

"If

"If there be (faith the Mofaic code) among you a poor man, of thy brethren, thou fhalt not harden thy heart, nor fhut thine hand from thy poor brother." If thou forbear, fays Solomon, to deliver him that is ready to be flain, and fay, "Behold, I knew it not;" doth not he that pondereth the heart confider it? and he that keepeth thy foul, doth not he know it? and will not he render to every man according to his works?

If a felfifh fpirit be thus foolifh, contemptible, unjuft, and impious, with what caution ought we to refift the firft advances of this temper! with what diligence fhould we cultivate the contrary habits of benevolence and generofity! There is, I truft, little danger, with refpect to any of us, of fuffering the felfifh paffions to degenerate into fuch a dreadful ftate of malignity, as to render us capable of committing the fhocking crime, which the interrogation of the text was intended to conceal. Be it remembered, however,

however, that the most atrocious depravity of character commonly originates in selfishness. Had Cain loved his brother as he ought, he had been incapable of lifting up his hand against him. But the want of affection produced neglect: neglect opened the door to jealousy and envy: envy settled into malice, and malice made Cain a murderer.

When you first suffer your benevolent affections to sleep for want of exercise, and indulge a selfish humour, you may probably see little reason to be apprehensive of danger. No other effect may, perhaps, be visible, than some degree of languor, or interruption, in your performance of social duties. You are, it is true, less industrious than formerly, to discover, and less anxious to relieve, objects of compassion; you are less assiduous in serving your friends, less solicitous to keep up those courteous and kind attentions towards your relations and intimate

mate connexions, which are the food of affection, or less active and zealous in prosecuting useful designs. But, as all these are mere *omissions*, they give you little alarm. The gradual change in your disposition either passes without notice, or is ascribed to some cause with which your character has no concern. Be upon your guard, however, against the first appearance of evil. The transition from the omission of accustomed expressions of kindness to the commission of actual offences against justice and humanity is not difficult. The same selfish spirit which led you to the former, may, if you continue to indulge it, urge you on to the latter. In proportion as you lose your inclination to serve others, by the occasional sacrifice of your time, your pleasures, or your wealth, to their benefit, you will become inclined to sacrifice their convenience, their peace, and their dearest rights, to your own interest. As the desire of doing good decreases, the love of gain will increase: and it will be impossible to say, to what " deceits of unrighteousness," to what cruelties of oppression, you may at length be able to reconcile yourself, in order to increase your possessions. The passions of the human heart, like the waters of the ocean, are never at rest. When the benevolent affections are suffered to subside, the selfish passions will of course become predominant, and every fatal consequence of their indulgence is to be dreaded.

The only effectual security against these evils is the diligent cultivation and daily exercise of that charity which " seeketh not its own profit, but the profit of many." Accustom yourselves to take a warm and affectionate interest in the happiness of all around you. Give up your hearts in cordial attachment to those who have a just claim to your love. Seek, and you will not fail to find, your highest

highest pleasure in obliging them. Make their sorrows, as well as their joys, your own; and take pains to alleviate the one, and heighten the other, by unaffected kindness and active generosity.

Having discharged these first offices of love, look beyond your domestic circle; and observe what passes in your neighbourhood, not to feed a censorious humour with daily tales of scandal, but to furnish your generosity with continual opportunities of useful exertion. Approve yourselves good citizens, by interesting yourselves in every event which affects the prosperity of your country, and by cheerfully affording your countenance and support to designs which promise to relieve its burdens, improve its commerce, reform its police, extend its liberties, and promote its welfare. In fine, enlarge your views, and cherish your philanthropy, by remarking, with interested attention, every change which is taking place in the civil and religious ſtate of the world, every effort which is making towards relieving ſociety from the burden of oppreſſion, and the human mind from the dominion of prejudice. Conſider yourſelves as citizens of the world; regard all mankind as your brethren; and ſay with the ancient Poet*,

"I am a man; and nothing is indifferent to me which concerns the human kind."

---

* Homo ſum, nihil humanum a me alienum puto.

Characters of Charity.

1 Cor. xiii. 4, 5.

Charity suffereth long, and is kind; charity envieth not; charity vaunteth not itself, is not puffed up; doth not behave itself unseemly; seeketh not her own; is not easily provoked; thinketh no evil.

The Christian religion is justly characterised as the religion of love; and is on this account frequently, and very deservedly, made the theme of high panegyric. But the peculiar excellence of Christianity, considered under this particular aspect, will be more distinctly perceived, if the several lineaments and features

tures of the Divine form of Christian charity be accurately examined; if the powerful and extensive influence of this principle upon the temper and conduct of those in whom it is predominant be attentively observed. And in prosecuting this inquiry we cannot follow a better clue, than that which the apostle Paul has furnished in that beautiful and judicious description of its leading characters, given in the memorable passage, of which my text is the first part. Let us examine each of the properties of charity, here enumerated, as far as they are distinctly marked, in order to discover the grounds of each character, and to be convinced of the excellence of the principle to which it is ascribed.

As things are only to be defined by their properties, it is not easy to give an accurate definition of charity, which will not include some of the characters laid down by the apostle. It may be sufficient

cient to say in general, that by charity we understand an inward principle of good-will, which inclines a man to desire and pursue the happiness of others.

Concerning this principle, the apostle teacheth, in the first place, that it " suffereth long."

Long-suffering supposes the repeated or continued endurance of inconvenience, hardship, or injury, from others. And in the present state of things it is impossible not to meet with a variety of lesser vexations, or more serious sufferings, from the inadvertencies, the capricious humours, or the criminal passions, of those with whom we are connected. A selfish man, who has no other views than his own ease and gratification, only considering how much these cross accidents interrupt his personal enjoyment, will be restless and fretful under them, and will have no patience either to endure smaller inconveniencies till they can be easily and

quietly

quietly remedied, or to wait for the redrefs of greater evils, till prudence and calm reflection have fuggefted the fafeft and moft equitable method of proceeding. But let a man be infpired with the divine fpirit of charity, and he will inftantly become poffeffed of a new fet of motives for forbearance, to which thofe who " live to themfelves" are entire ftrangers. Looking around him upon his brethren with an eye of good-will, he regards them as alike entitled with himfelf to a fhare of happinefs, and alike furrounded with difficulties and obftructions in the purfuit. If their humours and paffions fometimes interfere with his comfort, he candidly reflects, that probably his may alfo fometimes interfere with theirs. Or, whether the account be in this way exactly balanced or not, he is fenfible that many of the infelicities of which he complains arife from the common frailties of human nature, againft which it does not

become

Characters of Charity. 155

become a human being to exercife feverity. When the opinion or the inclination of a friend or relative thwarts his own, when even his wayward humour proves troublefome to him, the goodnefs of his heart enables him to find more pleafure in filent acquiefcence or placid fubmiffion than in vehement contradiction. He has too much regard for the peace and comfort of thofe he loves, as well as for his own, to be pertinacious in trifles; and efteems a fmall facrifice of inclination or judgment well repaid by the prefervation of mutual good humour and affection. In more important concerns, where he judges it neceffary, after much forbearance, to feek relief from fufferings, or redrefs for injuries, he will permit no unneceffary feverity to darken his proceedings, no thirft of revenge to inflame his bofom. If he reprove, it will be in the fpirit of meeknefs; if he punifh, it will be with as much lenity as

will

will be confiftent with his own fafety, and the intereft of fociety. In fine, charity will enable a man, in the moft trying fituations, to bear with the prejudices, frailties, and perverfe humours of others; at all times to refrain from revenge; and fo be ready to exercife a forbearing and forgiving fpirit towards his greateft enemies. Who can doubt that fuch a temper muft be a perpetual fource of tranquil enjoyment to its poffeffor, and muft contribute, as far as it prevails, to the peace and happinefs of fociety?

In the fecond place, charity is KIND.

This character of charity reprefents, in the moft amiable light, both the difpofition in which the effence of this virtue confifts, and its external expreffions in words and actions. When good-will, grounded in principle and confirmed by habit, is accompanied with a natural fweetnefs of temper and tendernefs of heart, the refult is, the lovely quality of kindnefs, with all its pleafing and beneficial

ficial fruits. Where kindness is the prevailing disposition of the mind, it finds the most natural exercise and delightful employment of its affections in looking beyond itself to the condition of others; in rejoicing with them in their prosperity, and compassionating their sorrows; in cherishing and expressing a cordial attachment to relatives and friends, and a desire of obliging and serving them; and in " devising liberal things" for the relief of the poor and necessitous, or for the benefit of the public. Rich and plentiful are the streams which flow from the fulness of a kind heart. Kindness, thoroughly formed into the habit and temper of the soul, will spread a winning sweetness over the countenance, give a mild lustre to the eyes, call forth gentle and harmonious accents from the lips, and diffuse over the whole frame an air and manner more truly graceful than art alone could ever bestow. The great secret of being agreeable is to be kind. Studied charms and

graces

graces lose their effect as soon as it is perceived that they originate in vanity, and terminate in selfishness. But where the kind heart goes out of itself, and discovers a sincere desire of giving pleasure, or bestowing benefits, not for its own sake, but for the sake of the object of its kindness, the glow of affection which it communicates will not fail to be reflected back upon itself. The animated form does not differ more from the lifeless statue, than artificial politeness differs from real kindness: but it is not in its effect on the exterior, or in its influence on the comfort of social intercourse, that the chief value of this property of charity consists. Kindness is the first ingredient in domestic happiness: it is the quality which, above all others, renders husbands and wives, parents and children, dear to each other; which makes the labours, the cares, and the duties, of these relations easy; and which, in a word, blesses the habitation of the good. Kindness is

the

the parent of friendly, humane, and generous actions. It is this which, between friends, dictates the seasonable counsel, the mild rebuke, and the faithful admonition. It is this which, between superiors and inferiors, lessens the elevation of rank, and lightens the burdens of dependance. It is this which dictates words of comfort, and prompts to deeds of liberality, towards the necessitous and afflicted. In a word, it is kind charity which opens the heart to the whole human race, and which makes the performance of good actions, in every way which wisdom and discretion direct, a man's business and delight.

A third character of charity is, that it is free from envy. Charity ENVIETH NOT.

If the nature of envy be duly considered, it will appear that this malignant disposition takes its rise from selfishness, and consequently that its proper remedy, or preventative, is charity. Why does any one observe with secret uneasiness the rising

rising reputation of another? Why is he jealous of the distinction which the world seems inclined to bestow on his talents? When any one is praised for genius, learning, personal attractions, or elegant accomplishments, why is his praise sometimes heard with a reluctant ear? Whence the coolness with which people frequently give their assent to the commendation which they do not chuse to contradict, and the eagerness with which they seize an occasion of depreciating what they cannot directly blame? The reason undoubtedly is, that men in these cases perceive, or imagine, an interference with their own prospects of fame and distinction, and are restless under the apprehension of being eclipsed by the increasing splendour of others. In like manner, when persons in an inferior station of life look up with an evil eye to those who enjoy superior advantages of rank and fortune; when they scrutinise their actions with a malignant severity; when the bosom of an unsuccesful candidate for an honourable or lucrative station swells with indignation against the more fortunate competitor; when jealousies arise between rivals in trade, or among common adventurers in projects which promise a large return of honour or profit; the cause is still the same. Envy, under every aspect which it assumes, springs from that inordinate self-love which would gladly sacrifice to its own gratification every interfering interest. The proper cure of this wretched and troublesome temper is the cultivation of the benevolent spirit enjoined by Christianity in the divine precept—" Thou shalt love thy neighbour as thyself." The man who possesses this charitable disposition will be wholly incapable of fretting and murmuring at the prosperity of others, much less of exulting in their disappointments and mortifications. The generous affection with which he regards all mankind inclines him to rejoice in the prosperity of others,

others, and gives a kind of participation in their enjoyments, which is no small addition to his own share of felicity. In a heart expanded with sentiments of universal philanthropy, the success and reputation of another can excite no mean jealousy or restless spleen; for to such a heart another's happiness becomes, by generous sympathy, its own. Charity envieth not.

The apostle adds, Charity VAUNTETH NOT ITSELF, IS NOT PUFFED UP.

Pride and charity, or benevolence, are dispositions so contrary to each other both in their nature and effects, that in the proportion in which the one predominates in any heart, the other must be subdued. Pride is a selfish passion, fixing a man's attention upon his own accomplishments, or his own possessions, with a degree of complacency and admiration which leaves him little inclination to satisfy the equitable claims, or indulge the reasonable expectations of others. Those who think

of

of themselves more highly than they ought to think, will seldom think justly of the merit of other men, or be disposed to pay them deserved respect. Eager to obtain for themselves that degree of attention and applause which they judge to be due to their superior merit, but to which few besides themselves will think them entitled, they must unavoidably meet with frequent mortifications, which will put them out of humour with the world, and lead them to view the characters of others through the discoloured medium of spleen and ill-humour. Hence must unavoidably arise a settled disinclination to the exercise of kind affections, and to the performance of kind offices. On the contrary, where benevolence is the ruling principle, a generous attention to the inclinations and interests of others will find a man other occupation for his thoughts than that of brooding over his own fancied excellencies. A good man will find much more pleasure in paying the tribute of applause to another, than in extorting or courting it for himself. In the exercise of benevolence he will suffer none of the artificial distinctions of society to become a barrier between him and his fellow-creature. Before the genial influence of charity every cold obstruction of this kind melts away. To the truly charitable man every one to whom he can do an act of civility, or render a more substantial kindness, however inferior to him in rank or fortune, is his neighbour, friend, and brother. Charity is the parent of modesty. No man, who has a generous respect for the feelings of others, will make an ostentatious display of his superiority. True benevolence will dictate a delicate reserve, in the presence of inferiors, with respect to those advantages of mind, person, or fortune, a forward exhibition of which might give them the pain of an humiliating comparison. To avoid, as much as possible, whatever would render inferiors dissatisfied

fied with themselves and their condition; to treat them with easy affability, rather than distant condescension; to "instruct the ignorant, without upbraiding them with their defects;" to "supply the wants of the poor, without appearing to take notice of their poverty;" in a word, to do whatever can be done towards annihilating in the minds of those who are below us all uneasy apprehension of inferiority; are the lessons taught by that charity which " vaunteth not itself."

Whilst charity restrains and subdues pride, it of course checks indecorum and rudeness of manners: it DOTH NOT BEHAVE ITSELF UNSEEMLY.

The selfish passion of pride is one of the chief sources of unseemly incivility. Men think it beneath them to bestow attention upon those whom they despise; and there are comparatively few whom the proud man does not despise. Those whom he knows, or fancies to be his inferiors, such a man will not think it worth his while to treat with respect, unless it be to serve some private purpose. Nay, it is not uncommon for persons, who with conceit and vanity unite an unfeeling temper, to take pleasure in doing and saying offensive and unbecoming things. Nothing will so effectually correct every inclination of this kind, as admitting into the breast the gentle spirit of christian charity. The established forms of good-breeding, it is true, contribute much towards this end, by making every man's reputation and interest depend, in a great measure, upon the decency and civility of his deportment: but the only certain and universal check upon rude and unbecoming behaviour is a settled principle of good-will; for though this principle may not make a man an adept in the arbitrary rules of politeness, it will do what these can never accomplish; it will inspire him with a disposition to please and oblige, which will, in all societies and connections, preserve him from giving unnecessary

cessary offence. The general law—
"Thou shalt love thy neighbour," comprehends the particular precept—"Be courteous."

The next character of charity, laid down by the apostle in the text, is that essential quality which principally marks its general nature, *disinterestedness*. Charity SEEKETH NOT HER OWN.

There is no one trait of character which so completely as this distinguishes what is great and excellent from what is mean and despicable in moral temper and conduct. Wherever you find a man whose desires and pursuits all center in himself—in whose plan of life, kindness to friends, generosity to the public, liberality to the necessitous, has no share—who never assumes the semblance of these virtues but to answer some purpose of personal interest—it is impossible you should not contemplate his character with a mixture of aversion and contempt. But if, on the contrary, you observe any one rising above that sordid selfishness which lives only for itself, and enlarging his views, extending his desires, and directing his exertions, to the benefit of his particular connexions, of the community to which he belongs, and of the whole human species, the view of such a character naturally kindles in your breasts a glow of generous admiration. This essential difference in human characters arises solely from the presence or the absence of the divine principle of charity. Not that it is desirable, or possible, that any man should be indifferent to his own welfare. Every wise man will steadily pursue his own happiness, and in this sense " seek his own:" but if he, at the same time, be a good man, he will do more. Independently of all regard to himself, he will sincerely desire, and earnestly endeavour, to promote the welfare of others. His life will be enriched and adorned with a series of kind, humane, and generous actions; and in performing them his attention

tention will be wholly directed towards the objects of his beneficence. He will indeed derive pleasure of the purest and most exalted kind from seeing the fruits of his goodness: but it will not be the hope of obtaining this pleasure which will be his immediate object. Forgetting himself, he will do good for the sake of making others happy, and purely because he loves them. In actually increasing the happiness of another, he attains the ultimate object of his wishes: for in all his good actions he seeks not his own profit, or the gratification of his own vanity, but the profit of another, that he may be relieved from some infelicity, or, may receive some addition to his stock of enjoyment. Where the heart is full of kindness the hand will be ready to every good work.

Of charity the apostle saith further, that **it is not easily provoked.**

From natural irritablity of temper, or from an habitual indulgence of the irascible

ble paffions, fome perfons are much more "eafily provoked" than others; but it is the natural effect of the principle of benevolence to reftrain and moderate the paffion of anger. This it will do two ways: Firft, by leading a man to behold all around him with that eye of kindnefs which will take more pleafure in dwelling upon the amiable qualities of others than their defects, and which will be more inclined to overlook trifling offences than to view them through the magnifying medium of ill-humour; and, fecondly, by rendering him more inclined to confult the peace and comfort of others by fubduing, than his own gratification in indulging, his refentment. With the fame natural temper the benevolent man finds fewer occafions of anger than the felfifh man: and when fuch occafions unavoidably arife, his benevolence will difpofe him to render his anger as little as poffible painful or troublefome to others. How amiable, how excellent, does the

spirit

spirit of charity appear, when we contemplate its wonderful power to soften the temper, to gentle the manners, and to render " man mild and sociable to man!" How greatly would the harmony of families and the peace of society be increased—how much more perfectly would mankind experience the pleasure and benefit of " living together in unity," if they were universally taught, by the law of charity, not to be " easily provoked!"

The last property of charity which I shall at present consider is, that it THINKETH NO EVIL.

This may either denote that charity renders men disinclined to think evil concerning the character and conduct of others, or that it prevents them from thinking or designing evil against others. The former explanation of the phrase would make it of the same import with a subsequent character of charity, that it " believeth all things, and hopeth all things."

I there-

I therefore underſtand it in the latter ſenſe, as implying that a man who is governed by the ſpirit of charity, will not be able to deviſe and purſue any meaſures which would be injurious to the peace and happineſs of his neighbour. And this is certainly a juſt and important character of charity; for it is very evident that the ſame ſpirit which diſpoſes a man to do good, muſt reſtrain him from doing evil. In a heart poſſeſſed and animated by love, there can be no room for malicious purpoſes, or treacherous and fraudulent deſigns. You will never find a truly benevolent man impoſing upon the credulous and unſuſpecting, or deceiving the ignorant, to ſerve his own lucrative ends; you will never find him taking advantage of inexperience and weakneſs to gratify his deſires; you will never find him invading the property or the liberty of his fellow-creatures, and ſubjecting them to involuntary ſufferings, for the ſake of increaſing his own wealth and ſplendour.

You

You may safely entruſt your moſt important concerns in his hands; for his benevolence will effectually preſerve him from wronging you, even in circumſtances in which he might do it with perfect ſecreſy and ſecurity. In fine, benevolence is, in all the tranſactions of ſocial life, the ſureſt guard of juſtice and equity. "Love worketh no ill to his neighbour; therefore love is the fulfilling of the law."

Characters of Charity.

1 Cor. xiii. 6—8.

Charity rejoiceth not in iniquity, but rejoiceth in the truth; beareth all things; believeth all things; hopeth all things; endureth all things: charity never faileth.

THE characters of charity which have already passed under our notice are, that it exercises patient forbearance under injuries—that it cherishes kind affections, and delights in kind actions—that it subdues the tormenting passion of envy—that it banishes pride from the heart, and prevents indecorum and rudeness of manners—that it raises the soul above the meanness of selfishness, and dictates disinterested acts of beneficence—that it restrains and moderates the passion of anger

anger—and that it renders thofe who are under its influence incapable of forming defigns injurious to the welfare of others. "Charity fuffereth long, and is kind; charity envieth not; charity vaunteth not itfelf, is not puffed up; doth not behave itfelf unfeemly; feeketh not her own; is not eafily provoked; thinketh no evil." It now remains, that we contemplate this divine virtue, as the admirer and friend of merit; as the candid apologift for human infirmity; as a patient and hardy fufferer for the benefit of mankind; and as poffeffing within itfelf a principle of immortality. Charity "rejoiceth not in iniquity, but rejoiceth in the truth; beareth all things, believeth all things, hopeth all things, endureth all things; charity never faileth."

It has been ufual with moral writers to fpeak of virtue under the appellation of *Truth*: and fome moralifts have proceeded fo far as to maintain, that there is no

no term which more accurately expresses the nature and ground of moral obligation. It has been observed in support of this opinion, that actions have a language as intelligible and precise as words, and that whenever a man acts virtuously he conforms to the real nature of things, and consequently in effect gives his assent to some truth; but that, on the contrary, whenever a man is guilty of any immoral action, he contradicts some known and established truth, and virtually asserts a falsehood. If this speculation should be thought too refined, it will not admit of dispute, that there is an analogy between truth and virtue, arising from the conformity of both to nature and reason, which justifies the metaphorical application of the term truth to moral conduct. Upon the ground of this analogy doubtless it is, that our Saviour speaks of " doing truth." " Every one that doth truth cometh to the light." And in this
sense

sense the word *truth* seems to be used by the Apostle in the text, in which *truth* is opposed to iniquity: " rejoiceth not in iniquity, but rejoiceth in the truth."

The character of charity expressed in these words is, then, that it forbids all malicious exultation in the folly and misconduct of others, and disposes the mind to feel a generous satisfaction in contemplating their virtues. Where a genuine and ardent spirit of benevolence is united with a strong conviction of the importance of virtue to the happiness of a rational being, it will be impossible to behold the vices of individuals, or the general prevalence of wickedness in the world, without emotions of regret and sorrow. To see men, whose capacities and situations have afforded them every advantage for attaining a distinguished and happy station in society, blotting the page of their fair fame with dishonourable deeds, and by their indiscretions and follies

lies blighting in the blossom the rich fruits of happiness, present and future. To survey a race of beings, whom the Author of their nature has furnished with noble faculties, and inspired with immortal hopes, degrading themselves by foolish and base pursuits; tormenting and plundering each other to become possessed of wealth, which they know not how to use and enjoy; and forfeiting their title to future felicity by abusing the present gifts of Divine Providence; must be painful to a generous mind. Every one whose bosom glows with the genuine sentiments of piety and humanity will be inclined, on such a survey, to adopt the language of David, " I beheld the transgressors and was grieved." A temper the reverse of this, which is capable of contemplating the vices of mankind with pleasure, and " rejoicing in iniquity," implies a depth of depravity which, for the honour of human nature, one would gladly

gladly suppose to have no other existence than in the ideal character of that personified principle of evil, who, in the language of poetry, says to Evil, "Be thou my good." But though such diabolical malignity as this is not, it may be hoped, often found in a human breast, yet it is, perhaps, no uncommon thing for men, through a selfish inattention to whatever lies beyond the narrow circle of their own affairs, or possibly through mere indolence, to be wholly indifferent to the state of morals and religion in the world around them. It requires some enlargement of understanding, as well as generosity of spirit, to be able to survey the world with that interested attention to its moral state which will dispose us to "rejoice in the truth." In proportion, however, to the degree in which our minds are enlightened with just views, and our hearts are enriched with generous sentiments, will be our progress in that sublime philanthropy which, estimating the progress of mankind towards perfection, by the advances which they make in virtue, exults in every appearance of moral improvement as a pledge of good to the whole human race.

The same principle, exercised upon individual objects within the sphere of our personal connexions, will lead us to mourn over the failings, and to observe with delight the excellencies of our acquaintance and friends. Instead of exulting, with the malicious and envious, in the sudden fall of any distinguished character; instead of dwelling with eager satisfaction on the particulars of his disgrace, we shall lament it with unaffected regret, both on account of the personal infelicity which it occasions, and the discredit which it brings upon the cause of virtue. Wherever examples of singular merit are exhibited—wherever actions highly meritorious are performed; despising

spising the pitiful jealousy which would incline us to be silent concerning excellencies which we have not resolution and virtue enough to emulate, we shall dwell with delight upon the contemplation of such exalted characters, and gladly embrace every opportunity of holding them up to the view of others. And this tribute we shall pay to superior merit, not from the selfish wish of sharing its lustre by reflection, but from an honest desire of rendering honour to whom honour is due, and from the generous motive of serving mankind by exciting a laudable spirit of emulation.

The next character of charity, given in the text, according to our translation, is, that it "beareth all things." But the most usual signification of the original word here rendered *beareth*, is *covereth*; and this interpretation furnishes a character of charity entirely distinct from the rest, yet easily connected with those that immediately

immediately follow; whereas the clause, as it is given in our translation, is in meaning a repetition of the first clause, "charity suffereth long." I therefore read the passage—charity *covereth* all things, and understand it in the same sense in which I conceive the maxim of the apostle Peter is to be understood, "Charity covereth, or hideth a multitude of sins;" that is, it is the office of charity to cast a veil over the faults of others, which may as much as possible hide them from public view. And this must be acknowledged to be an important branch of the duty enjoined upon Christians in the new commandment, that they should love one another. Considering what an imperfect and erring race of beings we are, and how liable the best among us might be to just censure, and, perhaps, in some sort, even to disgrace, were all our little foibles and failings and trespasses industriously collected,

and

and on every occaſion ſtrictly canvaſſed, the common practice of talking of other men's faults is not very prudent. But whatever may be thought of the diſcretion, or the utility of this practice, certainly very little can be ſaid in behalf of its benevolence. Thoſe whoſe daily employment it is to retail idle ſtories of detraction, even though they be founded in truth, without having any other end to anſwer by ſuch converſation, than merely to amuſe themſelves and their friends, will not find it an eaſy taſk, wholly to exculpate themſelves from the charge of malignity and ill-nature. For it is impoſſible, upon theſe occaſions, to liſten to the whiſpers of benevolence, without immediately perceiving, that there is much unkindneſs in unneceſſarily expoſing to view the failings of perſons who are guilty of no heinous crimes, and are perhaps, in other reſpects, entitled to much eſteem. Charity, inſtead of permitting

mitting us to indulge ourselves in wanton sarcasms or rigorous censures, will teach us to discountenance these practices in others by giving their censorious tales a cool reception, by vindicating, as far as we are able, the character which is severely treated; and where an entire exculpation is impossible, by generously bringing into view, by way of pleasing contrast, its merits and amiable qualities; hereby *hiding* or *covering*, as far as we are able, a multitude of faults.

In forming a judgment of the actions and characters of others, charity will teach us to pay a willing attention to every circumstance which may serve to weaken the credit of an ill report, or to extenuate the fault which cannot be concealed. Charity " believeth all things, hopeth all things." It is a common practice, and indeed a very natural method of proceeding, for men to measure others by themselves. Those who are conscious

conscious of little excellence in their own dispositions and characters, will scarcely be able to persuade themselves that any such thing as disinterested and exalted merit is to be found in the world. Those who harbour in their own bosoms dark purposes, mean sentiments, and malignant passions, will naturally suspect that others do the same. Hence they will eagerly seize upon any tale, however improbable, which may serve to cast a shade over distinguished merit, and entertain any suspicion, however groundless, rather than suppose it possible, that any character can exist which is far superior to their own. Looking with an eye of distrust and jealousy upon every appearance of virtue, they are always ready to discover some bad motive in every good action, and to insinuate a charge of hypocrisy against the most upright and excellent man. On the contrary, the man who is conscious of nothing but honest intentions and generous purposes, will expect

to

to find in others the same integrity and benevolence which he himself possesses; and will not easily persuade himself to believe that there is so much fraud and wickedness in the world as many suppose. If experience obliges him to lower the favourable opinion which artless honesty and unsuspecting good-nature may have led him to entertain of mankind; if he find it necessary for his own security to guard against that easy credulity which is imposed upon by every specious pretence; he will, nevertheless, always be more inclined to err on the side of candour, than on that of severity.

This amiable virtue of candour can spring from no other source than a benevolent heart. Politeness may instruct a man to disguise his real sentiments concerning others; and a selfish desire of pleasing may induce him to lavish fulsome praise upon those whom in his heart he despises: but it is benevolence alone which

which can difpofe him to think as favourably of others as circumftances will permit, to pay a voluntary tribute of refpect to merit in obfcurity, and to make generous allowances for human imperfections. Let your bofoms be truly poffeffed with that charity which believeth all things and hopeth all things, and you will be more inclined to think well, than to think ill of others; you will take pleafure in contemplating the virtues of a character, though mixed with many imperfections. Where the general tenor of a man's conduct is good, you will not be difpofed, on account of a few cafual errors, to call in queftion his fincerity. If you fee any one regular in the performance of religious duties, you will give him credit, unlefs his actions directly contradict his profeffions, for fincere piety. When you obferve a man on all occafions liberal in his contributions towards the fupport of charitable eftablifhments, you will not eafily fufpect that his

his beneficence is the mere effect of vanity and oftentation. You will believe every man to be as virtuous as he appears, till you have undoubted proof to the contrary; and will not liften to fecret whifpers and dark fuggeftions, to the difadvantage of any one of whom you have hitherto feen reafon to entertain a favourable opinion. Even where circumftances arife which afford juft ground of fufpicion, you will not be hafty to judge, and will require full evidence before you condemn. As long as any juft ground of doubt remains refpecting the truth of the accufation, you will keep your judgment undecided; while you are deliberating upon the matter, you will be inclined to attend to every circumftance which may either refute the charge, or extenuate the offence: and even when you muft condemn it, it will be with regret, and without any unneceffary feverity. In this manner you will treat
the

the character, not of an indifferent perfon alone, but of your opponent, your rival, or your enemy; for, in thefe cafes, you will exercife more than ufual caution, left felf-love, jealoufy, a party-fpirit, or refentment, fhould bias your judgment, and lead you to pronounce an uncandid and unrighteous fentence. In a word, you will conftantly view the actions of men through the tranfparent medium of candour, and in the clear funfhine of good-nature, and confequently be always difpofed to form the moft favourable judgment concerning them. To convince you of the value of that candid temper which "believeth all things and hopeth all things," I need only for a moment turn your attention to the mifchiefs which the contrary fpirit is continually producing. To what muft we afcribe thofe daily flanders which are circulated with fuch eagernefs, and which meet with fuch a ready reception, in fociety?

ciety? Why is many a fair reputation blackened by fly infinuations and obfcure hints, unfupported by any fufficient proofs? Why are trifles light as air fo often allowed, in the decifions we pafs upon the characters of others, to have all the weight of the moft decifive evidence? Whence does it fo frequently happen, that trivial offences, mifreprefented by ill-nature, or mifapprehended by refentment, are often magnified into unpardonable affronts or injuries, and become the foundation of violent quarrels and implacable enmities, and perhaps the occafion of ruinous litigations, or fatal combats? Whence all this, but from that cenforious fpirit which eagerly takes up a reproach againft its neighbour, and " maketh a man an offender for a word?" Let it not then be thought furprifing, that this fpirit is fo feverely condemned by a religion, which is defigned to bring peace on earth, and to manifeft good-will towards men: and let it ever be regarded as an important part of that obedience which we owe to the law of Chriſt, to be candid in judging of each others characters. " Judge not, that ye be not judged."

It is in the next place aſſerted in the text, concerning charity, that it " endureth all things," by which phraſe, to diſtinguiſh it from the firſt character given of charity, " that it ſuffereth long," we muſt underſtand, that it inſpires fortitude in the execution of benevolent purpoſes. And this is a property of charity which greatly enhances its value and increaſes its utility. Charity may be conſidered as " enduring all things," either with reſpect to individual objects of benevolent affection, or with reſpect to mankind in general, and the great cauſe of virtue and religion. In the former point of view its beneficial effects are ſeen in a thouſand friendly exertions, attended with perſonal inconvenience and hazard, for the benefit of others. With the charitable

ritable man it is a first principle, that "no man liveth to himself." In the daily intercourses of domestic and friendly society this amiable spirit will dictate innumerable kind compliances with the inclinations of others, and friendly acts of civility for their accommodation, which necessarily imply, on the part of the agent, some sacrifice of personal ease and convenience. On more important occasions it will prompt the most active and resolute exertions for the benefit of those in whose welfare we take a generous interest. It is this which supports kind and affectionate parents under all the labour and anxiety and self-denial which they endure for the sake of their offspring; which inspires the humane and public-spirited friend of the poor with vigour and generosity to plan and execute designs for their benefit; which, in private friendship, renders a man capable of submitting to any expence or hazard in the service of those whom he loves. Among the

the charitable there may be found noble spirits who would not scruple to expose their lives in the defence of a valued friend. "Peradventure for a good man some would even dare to die." Where the object of generous exertions is the public benefit, a truly great and good man, actuated by a genuine spirit of philanthropy, will bid defiance to danger and to death. Such was the effect of the divine spirit of Christian charity upon the first disciples of Christ. Not a few among them exhibited, in their firm adherence to the cause of Christianity in the midst of severe persecution, an illustrious comment on St. Paul's precept to Timothy: "Thou therefore endure hardness as a good soldier of Jesus Christ." But no one ever displayed a brighter example of that fortitude which Christian benevolence inspires, than the apostle Paul himself. In the immediate prospect of bonds and afflictions he was able to say, "None of these things move me, neither count I my life dear unto me, that I may finish my course with joy, and the ministry which I have received of the Lord Jesus." And the same benevolent spirit, accompanied with just and enlarged views of the interest of mankind, has in almost every succeeding age produced men whose heroic exertions in the cause of humanity, virtue, or religion, have rendered them blessings to the world. To break the heavy yoke of oppression, to burst asunder the chains of slavery, to set the free-born mind at liberty from the bondage of superstition, to bless those who have dwelt in the dark regions of ignorance and error with the light of heavenly truth, are noble designs, in the prosecution of which there have not been wanting, and still are not wanting, great and generous spirits, who have the courage to despise obloquy, and to meet persecution without dismay. It is charity which creates martyrs, heroes, and friends of mankind. " Charity endureth all things."

The apostle closes his enumeration of
the

the amiable properties and happy effects of charity by adding, that it "never faileth." It accompanies the good man through every stage of his progress in virtue, grows with his growth, as he advances towards perfection, constitutes the principal part of his excellence, and, when he leaves this world, attends him to another, and becomes to him an eternal source of felicity. When he shall enter upon his everlasting inheritance, the faith and the hope which have assisted him in preparing for it will disappear; faith being exchanged for sight, and hope for possession: but charity is not only a necessary preparation for eternal happiness, but a principal ingredient in it, without which it is impossible that even the society of heaven should be a scene of enjoyment. Good men will hereafter enjoy uninterrupted felicity in each other's society, because they will be made perfect in love. "Charity never faileth."

After this distinct survey of the excellent properties and happy effects of charity, what further needs be added to engage every one, who is desirous of rendering himself amiable and useful to his fellow-creatures, or of obtaining the favour of that great and good Being, " who is love," to cultivate this virtue by every means in his power?—Knowledge and learning may excite admiration; power may command homage and subjection; wealth may procure you external tokens of respect, and give you rank and distinction in society; but it is charity or benevolence alone, which will afford you the pleasing consciousness of merit in your own bosoms, and obtain the cordial esteem and affection of mankind. A tenacious adherence to certain articles of religious belief, and a scrupulous observance of certain religious forms and ceremonies, may rank you among the members of this or that religious sect; but it is only an uniform obedience to that new commandment

commandment which Chrift hath given us, which can entitle you to the character of Chriftians. In the Chriftian church, which is founded in love, though we have all knowledge, and all gifts, if we have not charity we are *nothing*. Above all things, then, follow after charity, which is the bond of perfection; and may the God and father of our Lord Jefus Chrift make you to increafe and abound in love one towards another, and towards all men, to the end that your hearts may be eftablifhed unblameable in holinefs, and that ye may be prepared for an everlafting abode in the regions of perfect love and peace! Amen.

The good Man secure from Shame.

PSALM cxix. 6.

Then I shall not be ashamed, when I have respect unto all thy commandments.

THAT even virtuous and good men are wholly exempted from the painful feeling of shame, is more than can with truth be asserted. In the present state of society, we not only see shame incurred by such violations of decorum as imply no infringement of morality, but may not unfrequently observe men ashamed even of their virtues. Many persons, whose consciences will not suffer them to follow a multitude to do evil, nevertheless want courage sufficient to avow their good principles in the society of the licentious,

centious, and are afraid to be thought by their companions as virtuous and religious as they really are. This kind of timidity is at best a false modesty, which implies a culpable weakness of mind, and inconsistency of character: for it is impossible that virtue, which is in its nature the highest ornament and excellence of a rational being, and which is esteemed, by all who are capable of forming a judgment, the first object of admiration and love, should ever be dishonourable to those who practise it. Whatever ridicule men of corrupt principles and abandoned manners may affect to cast upon the conscientious and religious part of mankind, " wisdom will," in the issue, " be justified of all her children:" and though good men themselves may sometimes so far yield to the torrent of false opinion as to be ashamed of their goodness, they will at length lift up their heads with confidence in the sight of the wicked; for the memorial of virtue is immortal, and its triumph remaineth for ever. "Then shall I not be ashamed," saith the Psalmist, "when I have respect unto all thy commandments."

The doctrine which is implied in these words, and which will be the subject of the present discourse, is, that the man who faithfully obeys the will of God is free from all just occasion of shame. To illustrate this point, let us distinctly consider the light in which such a man's character appears to his OWN mind, to his FELLOW-CREATURES, and to his MAKER.

The man who religiously respects and diligently obeys the commands of God, has no secret consciousness of guilt to harass his mind, and render reflection a painful task. He is under no necessity of flying to scenes of dissipation and folly, as a shelter from the darts of an accusing conscience. He can endure and even enjoy solitude; and, without any foreign aid, can make himself happy in "communing with his own heart." If he reflect

flect upon the temper and habit of his mind, he has the satisfaction to be conscious, that whatever evil inclinations may have occasionally arisen within his bosom, his heart is on the whole sincerely disposed towards that which is good. If he review his actions, he has the comfort to find, that though he may, in some instances, have been betrayed into unbecoming conduct, the general tenor of his life has been conformable to the dictates of reason and the laws of religion. Having, therefore, no secret crimes to raise up, like spectres, before his imagination, solitude and darkness have for him no terrors. Conscious of his innocence and integrity, and of the virtuous state of his mind, he is, in the absence of all the world, " satisfied from himself."

It is a peculiar felicity attending the good man, that he has no occasion to have recourse to any of those arts of vanity, or subterfuges of hypocrisy, by means of which men of a contrary character often

impose

impose upon themselves as well as others. Being under no necessity to "deceive his own heart," he feels no inclination to gloss over his faults with fair names, or impute his good actions to better motives than belong to them. He neither brings forward the follies and vices of his neighbours as a foil to his own character; nor builds his good opinion of himself merely upon the reputation which he may have acquired among men, who can only judge of characters from external appearance. Listening with attention to the impartial decision of conscience, directed solely by the law of reason and the word of God, he passes sentence upon himself accordingly. Far from being ashamed or afraid to look into his own heart, he applies with diligence to the important office of self-inspection; and gladly avails himself of every aid which he can derive from the counsels and admonitions of friendship, from public instruction, or from the holy Scriptures.

Divesting

Divesting himself, as much as possible, of every bias which might lead him to make a precipitate or erroneous judgment, and endeavouring by every means in his power to furnish himself with an accurate knowledge of his duty, he honestly compares what he has been, with what he ought to have been, that he may make a true estimate of his moral and religious character. Having no secret forebodings that a fair inquiry will have an uncomfortable issue, he has no wish to conceal from his own observation any part of his character, but brings all his actions and designs under a fair and impartial examination. "He that doth truth," saith our Saviour, "cometh to the light, that his deeds may be made manifest that they are wrought in God." The result of this fair and equitable trial is, that the good man enjoys the testimony of his conscience, "that in simplicity and godly sincerity he has had his conversation in the world." And the well-founded persuasion

sion which he enjoys of the uprightness of his intentions, and the general goodness of his character, disposes him to relish the enjoyments of life with the highest satisfaction, enables him to endure its troubles with calmness and fortitude, and prepares him to leave the world in peace, and to enter upon a future state with a joyful hope of everlasting life.

As the man who has respect to all the commands of God is not ashamed to look inward upon *himself*, so neither is he ashamed to have his character and conduct exposed to the view of the world.

Few persons, indeed, have attained to such excellence of character as not to be conscious of many imperfections, which, were they laid open before the world, would, in some measure, tarnish the reputation they have acquired: and they who are most solicitous to possess distinguished merit, being above all others attentive to their own dispositions and conduct, are most of all sensible of their deficiencies.

ficiencies. Such men will not, therefore, obtrude their characters, with ostentatious confidence, upon the public eye; but, from a consciousness that they have honestly endeavoured to deserve the good opinion of the world, they can meet its inspection without any painful apprehension for the result. Whilst those who have a secret conviction that they are pretending to virtues to which they have no just claim, and imposing upon the world by assuming the semblance of goodness, at the same time that they are strangers to the reality, must be perpetually depressed by a degrading consciousness of unworthiness, and ashamed to lift up their faces in the presence of honest and good men; they, on the contrary, who are able to reflect, that in all the relations and concerns of life they have maintained a conscience void of offence, and done to others as they would have others do to them, have within themselves a firm foundation of confidence, and may on all

occasions

occasions stand forth to public view without dismay.

To be convinced of the unspeakable advantage which the honest and good man has in this respect over the knave and hypocrite, view him in several distinct capacities and relations, to remark what unaffected courage and confidence the consciousness of acting and meaning well inspires.

Observe him in commercial life, and you will see that, having never wronged or defrauded any man, but always acted upon the principles of the strictest equity and nicest honour, he is not afraid of meeting with a single individual, where-ever he goes, who can upbraid him with having imposed upon his ignorance, or abused his confidence. He never sees the man who calls to his remembrance acts of dishonesty or meanness which he would be ashamed to bring to light; or has occasion to impute it to his good fortune, that he has escaped the neglect and contempt,

tempt, or the punishment, which he has merited. Every one with whom he has transacted business is a witness to his fair and honourable proceedings; and he can never want friends, who will take pleasure in advancing his prosperity, or in affording him assistance upon an unexpected reverse of fortune. The consciousness of his own integrity, and the reliance he places on the good opinion of mankind, accompany him wherever he goes, and inspire him with a degree of confidence, in the prosecution of his designs, which none but an honest man ever feel.

View him, in the next place, in the capacity of a friend. He has made no professions of friendship which his heart did not acknowledge: he has violated no engagement or promise; he has betrayed no secret with which confidence or friendship had entrusted him; he has never forgotten the zeal and tenderness which are due to the interest and character of a friend.

friend. He can therefore have no wish to conceal from his friend any part of his conduct, and is capable of enjoying in perfection all the delights of reciprocal attachment and confidence. Has he been appointed guardian of the fatherless, or protector of the widow? He has the satisfaction to reflect, that he has in no instance violated the sacred trust reposed in him, or, by abuse or delay, sacrificed the interests of his charge to his own; but, on the contrary, has, through the whole proceeding, faithfully discharged every obligation of equity and honour, of friendship and humanity. Far from feeling any shame or apprehension at the idea of having his whole conduct thoroughly canvassed, he feels a generous pride in the consciousness of having faithfully executed his trust, and finds a welcome testimony to his fidelity in the grateful hearts of the persons committed to his care. Accompany him into the retired scenes of domestic life, you will find that his character

racter will bear the strictest examination from those to whom it is most intimately known—you will see that, though he is obliged to solicit from the affection of his relatives and dependants a candid indulgence of his foibles and infirmities, he can make a confident appeal to them for the sincerity and ardour with which he has endeavoured to serve their interest and promote their happiness. Lastly, observe his works of charity and mercy, and you will find him reaping the fruits of his liberality in the gratitude of those whom his bounty has relieved, and in the esteem and affection of all the good around him: and though he has been influenced, in the distribution of his charity, by higher motives than the desire of applause, you will easily perceive that the remembrance of his generous deeds affords him satisfaction, and that the respect which they have procured him among his fellow-citizens inspires him with confidence.

So powerful is the effect of a consciousness

ness of having acted well with respect to mankind, that it even fortifies the mind against the malignant assaults of envy and slander. The fairest character may fall under reproach and obloquy, and may for a time lie under unjust censure. But the man who is conscious of his innocence, can be under no temptation to hide himself, at such a season, from the public eye, or to let the murmur against him die away without notice. This is, indeed, the wisest course which can be taken by those whose consciences second the public censure; and there are cases in which it may be most prudent to treat even slander and defamation with neglect. But honest and upright men have it commonly in their power to make their appeal to the public; and, by calling in the general testimony of their past conduct, as well as producing immediate evidence of their innocence, to silence the voice of slander.

In the last place, the good man has not only no reason for shame before men, but he he may also stand before the presence of his Maker and not be ashamed.

If we have sincerely and uniformly " had respect to the commandments of God," the reflection that he has been witness to our actions, though it may afford sufficient ground for humility, affords none for confusion or terror. The all-seeing God, who is perfectly acquainted with all our faults, likewise observes every secret tendency of the heart towards goodness, and will not suffer the meanest of his faithful servants to go without his reward. Our righteous and merciful Father observes with complacency every secret emotion of piety and benevolence, which has never appeared in action, to obtain approbation among our fellow-creatures; and we have the fullest assurance, that he who seeth in secret will reward us openly. If, therefore, we be conscious that our hearts are upright before God, we may derive the most solid support and comfort from the reflection, that he beholds and approves us. When we are retired from the world, we may rejoice in the presence of the Almighty, and esteem ourselves happy " that he sees our way, and counts all our steps."

To receive from the world a tribute of esteem, in recompence of real merit, must be highly grateful to every generous mind: but the highest reward we can receive on earth for the practice of exemplary virtues, is that of being able to look beyond the applauding multitude to him who searcheth the heart, and to entertain the persuasion, that the great Being, who is best able to form a true judgment of characters, beholds us with approbation and complacency.

If at any time we fail of meeting with that respect and kindness from our brethren which our conduct gives us a right to expect, we may console ourselves under undeserved neglect by appealing from the censorious and ill-judging multitude to the almighty Patron of virtue: we

may

may banish those painful feelings which calumny and slander naturally create in a good mind, by looking forward to the day when God will bring to light the hidden things of darkness, and make manifest the secrets of the heart; assuring ourselves that in that day of righteous retribution we shall have praise of God.

Possessed of the testimony of a good conscience, and able to say—"Remember, O Lord, how I have walked before thee in truth and with a perfect heart," we may look forwards to the final judgment of the world without confusion or dismay. The approbation of our own minds, grounded on an impartial examination of our characters, we may regard as the anticipation of our acquittal and acceptance in the presence of God: and this delightful expectation may be abundantly sufficient to support us under the troubles of life, and may enable us to see the time of our departure out of this life drawing nigh without alarm; and when it shall actually arrive, to commit ourselves into the hands of our faithful and merciful Creator, in humble hope of a resurrection into everlasting life. In that great day, when we shall be called from the dead to appear before the judge of all, and to receive according to the deeds done in the body, we shall have confidence and not be ashamed in his presence; we shall find, to our unspeakable and everlasting joy, that the sincerity and uprightness of our hearts, and the innocence and usefulness of our lives, are approved by our Almighty Sovereign; and we shall finally be admitted into his heavenly presence, to receive the end of our faith and hope, and the reward of our obedience, even the salvation of our souls.

Thus evident is it, that the man who hath respect to all the commandments of God hath no reason to be ashamed either within himself, before his fellow-creatures, or in the presence of his Maker.

What, my brethren, can more effectually

tually recommended to us a life of sincere and persevering obedience, than the doctrine which has now been established? To be able at all times to turn our thoughts upon ourselves with satisfaction, and enjoy the reflections of our own minds—to be capable of meeting the countenances of our fellow-creatures, whether friends or enemies, with modest confidence—to have it in our power, at all times, to lift up our eyes to our Maker with an humble hope of his approbation—to be under no painful apprehension from the censures of conscience, the opinion of the world, or the judgment of the Almighty, is surely the happiest condition of human beings in the present life. Who does not see that such a state of mind must be a source of substantial and permanent satisfaction, must yield the noblest support under all the distressing vicissitudes of this world, and must fortify the mind with the strongest consolation in the hour of death. Be it, then, our habitual care to walk before God in all his commandments and ordinances blameless, and to hold fast our integrity and not let it go, that our hearts may not reproach us as long as we live: for, " beloved, if our hearts condemn us not, then have confidence towards God."

Againſt Evil-ſpeaking.

TITUS iii. 2.

Put them in mind—to ſpeak evil of no man.

OF all the bad habits which we are liable to contract, perhaps there are none ſo hard to be cured, as thoſe which reſpect the tongue. The reaſon is, that we are much leſs apprehenſive of the criminality of words than of actions. Actions, which require more time, and are attended with a greater variety of circumſtances, force themſelves upon our obſervation, and impreſs our memories. "But words, which have wings," and fly away, ſlip from us unregarded, and the remembrance of them ſoon periſhes. Hence we are apt to look upon offences of the tongue as too trivial to merit any great degree of attention, and commit them, time after time, almoſt without notice; ſo that, before we are

aware,

aware, a criminal habit is formed. In this manner it is that men become habitual liars, swearers, and the like, without being sufficiently sensible of the guilt they are incurring, and perhaps almost without perceiving their faults. But there is no habit respecting the tongue, which steals more imperceptibly upon men than the habit of slander and detraction. There is, therefore, great necessity for a frequent repetition of those precepts which prohibit this vice—for " putting men in mind to speak evil of no man."

In the vice of evil-speaking we may remark three stages or degrees of criminality: the highest and most criminal, saying things to the injury or disadvantage of another which we *know to be false*; the *second*, spreading reports against another which we *do not know to be true*; the *third*, and lowest, speaking concerning the faults of others what we *certainly know*. Let us inquire into the degree of criminality attending each of these kinds of evil-speaking.

The

The man who, from his own wanton and wicked invention, expressly charges another with a crime or fault of which he knows him to be innocent, stands foremost in the rank of *evil-speakers*. When false accusations are brought forward publicly in a court of judicature, and asserted with the solemnity of an oath, the crime of slander, united with that of perjury, takes the deepest tincture of guilt. This most direct and heinous violation of the commandment—"Thou shalt not bear false witness against thy neighbour," is in all civil governments justly treated as an offence of the first magnitude. It implies a degree of depravity and malignity which excites universal indignation, and which, indeed, happily for mankind, is seldom found. In a less formal and public way it is, however, no very uncommon thing for people to bring false accusations against their neighbours. The love of truth, or the dread of the infamy of a lie, is often not sufficiently strong to fortify men against the temptations to slander, flander, which arife from a natural malignity of temper, from the occafional emotions of envy or refentment, from the violence of party fpirit, from vanity, or from mere wantonnefs. From fome one or other of thefe caufes it very frequently happens, that rumours to a man's difadvantage are not only eagerly feized and propagated, but wilfully and deliberately magnified. Nay, it cannot be doubted; for no other account can poffibly be given of many tales of fcandal which are in daily circulation—that there are not a few idle perfons in the world who, to exercife their ingenuity, or to gratify their fpleen, often employ themfelves in fabricating flanderous tales which are wholly without foundation. It was not without reafon admitted into the Mofaic law as an exprefs precept*—" Thou fhalt not raife a falfe report."

But there is fomething fo bafe and infamous in thefe direct attacks upon the characters of others, that thofe who are

* Exod. xxiii. 1.

Against Evil-speaking.

addicted to evil-speaking, for the most part, advance no further than to the *second degree* of the offence; and, without venturing positively to assert what they know to be false, content themselves with spreading reports, or insinuating hints, against their neighbours, which they *do not know* to be founded in truth.

Some people, in indulging their propensity to slander, have the prudence to confine themselves to general and indeterminate censures. Upon slight grounds of suspicion, which they would find it no easy matter to substantiate, they venture to call a man, in general terms, a hypocrite or knave, when they would not chuse to charge him with any direct acts of dishonesty. Such general reflections may, perhaps, tolerably well answer the purpose of their ill-nature, and will at the same time save them the trouble of bringing those proofs which might be expected in support of a more specific charge. With respect to the person accused, a general censure is, perhaps, more injurious than a para particular accusation, since it more easily obtains credit, and is with more difficulty refuted.

There are others, who, having formed a bad idea of the world from a few unlucky specimens, being naturally of a sour and morose disposition, or being conscious that they are themselves governed by unworthy principles, speak evil of others, by ascribing, without any sufficient reason, their good actions to bad motives. They allow, indeed, that *this* man is regular in his performance of religious duties, and *that* liberal in his contributions to public charities; but at the same time insinuate, that the one has some private vices which he wishes to conceal under the mask of piety, and that the other has some selfish ends to answer by an ostentatious display of munificence. There is a malignity in thus endeavouring, by groundless insinuations, to bring down the best characters to a level with the worst, which renders this kind of evil-speaking scarcely less criminal than lying slander.

Nearly akin to this is the common practice of putting an unfavourable conftruction upon words or actions which are of a doubtful nature. Wherever it may be eafily fuppofed that the perfon whofe conduct is cenfured may not have been culpable, to determine at once that he has been fo, without giving the matter a fair examination, is not only a breach of candour, but of juftice: it is cafting an odium upon his character, where, for aught that certainly appears, he might be entitled to acquittal, or perhaps to praife, and is therefore certainly to be guilty of the fecond kind of evil-fpeaking.

This charge muft alfo fall upon thofe who defignedly give partial and defective reprefentations of the conduct of others, concealing thofe circumftances which would place it in a favourable light, and infifting wholly upon fuch particulars as may ferve to make it appear culpable. Since it is impoffible that any caufe can be equitably determined without fairly hearing the evidence on both fides, he who,

who, in reporting a ſtory in which another's reputation is concerned, relates only the evidence againſt him, in effect ſlanders him.

Another ſpecies of evil-ſpeaking is that of bringing a charge againſt another upon ſlender evidence and uncertain conjecture. Every bare poſſibility, or faint appearance of probability, is not a ſufficient ground of accuſation. A man's fault ought, in common juſtice, to be fully proved before we ſuffer ourſelves to think, much more to ſpeak, ill of him. Whatever credit thoſe people, who detect the faults of others through a long train of ſuſpicions and conjectures, may gain for ſagacity and penetration, they will certainly have loſt the right to praiſe on the ſcore of candour. To liſten with greedy ears to every tale of ſcandal, to go up and down as a tale-bearer, to be induſtrious in circulating ſtories injurious to the characters of others, without inquiring after the authors of the report, or examining the probability of its truth and the evidence on which it rests, always betrays a vacant mind or a bad heart. So many proofs are daily arising of the uncertainty of common rumour, that every one who wishes to support any reputation either for charity and candour, or for prudence and good sense, will be cautious how he takes up a reproach against his neighbour. Whether an evil report be true or false, no man can have a right to give it his passport, till he has examined it.

Nor does it at all diminish the criminality of circulating reports, which, for aught that we certainly know to the contrary, may be false, that it is done, without any direct and positive assertions, by oblique insinuations and distant hints. Some busy detractors are, it is true, very ingenious in devising indirect methods of defamation. "How often," says an elegant writer*, " is the honesty and

---

* Sterne.

integrity of a man difpofed of by a fmile or a fhrug! How many good and generous actions have been funk into oblivion by a diftruftful look, or a myfterious whifper! How large a portion of reputation is fent out of the world by diftant hints, nodded away, and cruelly winked into fufpicion! How frequently does an innocent character bleed by a report, which the party, who is at the pains to propagate it, affects to mention with regret, and fcarcely to believe! Thefe invenomed arrows of defamation, fhot at random, and often in the dark, are perhaps not lefs fatal than the more direct attacks of that fword which has flain its thoufands and ten thoufands. In all thefe cafes the intention and the mifchief, and therefore the guilt, is the fame.

That evil-fpeaking, of the two kinds already infifted upon, is criminal, will be readily acknowledged. Every one who attends to the nature of the thing, or to the experience of the world, muft be be convinced, that slander is pernicious in its effects both with respect to the objects of defamation and the slanderer himself.

"A good name (saith Solomon) is rather to be chosen than great riches." So numerous are the pleasures and advantages attending a fair character, that there is no treasure which a wise man would resign with so much reluctance, excepting only his integrity. In robbing another of his good name you deprive him of the satisfaction which attends the consciousness of enjoying the approbation of the wise and good; you expose him to all the inconveniences of disgrace and infamy, whilst he ought to be experiencing the happy effects of a fair character. You weaken his influence, diminish his usefulness, impair his credit, and perhaps irreparably injure the fortunes both of the man himself and his posterity. The words of the slanderer are "all devouring words," his tongue is " a sword and sharp arrow."—" Many (saith the son of Sirach) have fallen by the edge of the sword, but not so many as have fallen by the edge of the tongue. Well is he that is defended from it, and hath not passed through the venom thereof; who hath not drawn the yoke thereof, nor been bound in its bands, for the yoke thereof is a yoke of iron, and the bands thereof are bands of brass: the death thereof is an evil death: the grave were better than it."

And the arrows which the slanderer casts upon others will, sooner or later, return upon his own head. It was the advice of the wise man, " Whether it be to a friend or foe, talk not of other men's lives; for he hath heard and observed, and when the time cometh he will shew his hatred." There is no injury which men resent with more indignation than that which is offered to their good name. If slander be not attended with more *fatal*

consequences

consequences (which, with modern notions of honour, will sometimes happen), it is sure to create ill-will and hatred in the person who suffers the injury; at the same time it cannot fail to excite suspicion, and provoke severity in others. The evil speaker gives those to whom he utters his slanders no favourable idea of himself. Were it not for the fond partiality which men have for themselves, few persons would be so blind as not to see, that the slanderer probably " speaks of them to others as he does of others to them." Indeed men are generally so apprehensive of the common danger arising from this practice, that they are generally careful enough to repay the slanderer in his own coin. There is scarcely any thing in which mankind practise more strict justice, than in " rendering evil for evil and railing for railing." It is a consideration of still greater moment, but surely not sufficiently attended to by those who with great pretensions to piety have not learned to keep their tongues from evil-speaking, that a habit of defamation implies a malignity of disposition wholly inconsistent with a religious character. "If any man among you seem to be religious and bridleth not his tongue, that man's religion is vain." "The mouth that slandereth slayeth the soul."

But the iniquity and folly of slander are too obvious to require further illustration. I therefore proceed, in the remainder of this discourse, to offer a few remarks on the *third* kind of evil-speaking, that which consists in saying what we certainly know to be true concerning the faults of others.

As this is a practice in which, to own the truth, all men more or less indulge themselves, it is but charitable to suppose that the world is not universally convinced of its criminality. And thus much must be acknowledged in excuse for the general practice, that there are some

some cases in which it is expedient and necessary, and others in which it is excusable and innocent, to speak of other men's faults.

It cannot be questioned, that, however disreputable the character of a public informer may be, it is a duty which every member of society owes to the state, to bring a legal accusation against such persons as have injured the community by any heinous violation of its laws. Philanthropy itself requires, that we should discover such offences as cannot be concealed without great injury or hazard to the public. A regard to the common good, or a desire of reforming an offender, or of rendering his offence useful to others, may justify a man in exposing many acts of dishonesty, treachery, or cruelty, which cannot be brought under the cognizance of the civil magistrate; in subjecting one who has been betrayed into unbecoming and culpable conduct to the wholesome discipline of reproof and censure, public or private, as the case may require; and in holding up the examples of bad characters, already commonly known to be such, as a caution and warning to the young and unexperienced. It is also an act of justice, which every one owes to himself, to bring deserved infamy upon another, in order to clear his own character from aspersion, or to obtain redress for any material injury which he may, in other respects, have suffered. And what in these cases we may justly and reasonably do in vindication of our own rights, we are certainly likewise at liberty to do in the service of a friend. Even without any such particular call of justice or friendship, where offences are notorious and scandalous, it would perhaps be too rigorous to require an entire concealment of the natural and laudable feelings of indignation and contempt. But where men's faults are not of such a nature as to require the interference of public justice,

tice, and render them altogether a disgrace to society, while they remain in a great measure unnoticed by the world, a much greater degree of caution and delicacy should be observed in speaking of them. Where any particular end, sufficiently important, can be answered by mentioning any one's faults—for instance, producing the amendment of the offender, or guarding those whom he might be in danger of seducing against the infection of his bad example—to take notice of them for these purposes, is not, in a culpable sense, evil-speaking. But it may be very justly questioned how far we ought to indulge ourselves in talking of the faults of others on the general principles, of exercising and improving our own moral taste and feelings, or dealing out a deserved portion of punishment to offenders. Let us for a moment examine each of these pleas for the common practice of making the faults and indiscretions of others the subject of conversation.

Nothing

Nothing certainly can be more commendable, than the cultivation of moral taste and sensibility. As in painting, or any other of the fine arts, so in morals, he who wishes to be an excellent performer himself, should often exercise his critical judgment and taste upon the productions of others. But, in criticising the *characters of others*, are we always sure that we are solely influenced by the laudable desire of improving our own? Have conceit and vanity no hand in drawing the comparison between our neighbour and ourselves? Do we take no ill-natured pleasure in exercising satirical humour and wit upon the faults or foibles which pass under our review? Are our censures of others never mixed with any degree of exultation in the idea, that their superiority over us in rank and fortune or accomplishments, is balanced by the degradation of their characters? In short, is it from the pure love of virtue that we censure vice? Is it from a laudable

able ambition of excelling in wisdom, that we despise and ridicule folly? If not, it may be fairly questioned whether our free criticisms upon others are, upon the whole, profitable to ourselves.

Shall this practice then be continued out of pure benevolence to the world? Will it be said, that what preachers call evil-speaking is an useful instrument for chastising folly and correcting vice; that the fear of what the world will say is one of the most powerful restraints upon excess; and that many irregularities are by this means prevented or corrected, which would elude every exertion of civil magistrates, or religious teachers? All this may perhaps, in part, be true: and were those who thus take upon them the character of censors, as much in earnest to discourage vice as they pretend to be; did they treat every kind of immorality with the contempt which it merits, and at the same time support their censures by an unblemished example in their own
conduct,

conduct, still greater benefit might be expected from their efforts in the cause of virtue. But taking the matter as it actually stands; whilst, in their strictures upon others, people evidently dwell with more pleasure upon their faults than their merits, and are more likely to irritate by the keenness of satire, than to reform by the gentleness of reproof; whilst, in cases where no injustice is intended, unnecessary and cruel severity is often exercised; and whilst, from various causes, there remains so much danger, that in evil-speaking men will pass over from truth to falsehood; it would perhaps be more advantageous than injurious to the interests of virtue, if it were adopted as a general rule, never to speak of other men's faults but on some just occasion, and for some good reason. This is a species of charity which we may exercise, as constantly as we please, without expence. "To speak well of others, as far as they deserve it, is an easy obligation, but not to speak *ill* requires only our silence, which costs nothing.

To conclude, if you wish to refrain from every culpable kind of evil-speaking, observe the following maxims:

When you are inclined to speak ill of any one, allow yourself time to reflect, whether you are certain of the truth of what you are disposed to say against him. This rule, strictly observed, would cut off " nine parts in ten of all the evil-speaking that is in the world." Ask yourself again, whether the person you are inclined to censure has not, on some occasion or other, done you a kindness for which you at least owe him the return of silence upon the subject of his failings. Consider further, whether you yourself are not liable to censure for the same fault, or some other of equal magnitude; and remember the doctrine of our Saviour, " He that is without sin let him cast the
first

first stone." Attend properly to your own characters and your own duty, and you will find little leisure for talking of other men's lives. To lessen your temptation to evil-speaking, cultivate your understandings, and by reading and reflection furnish yourselves with agreeable and useful topics of conversation. Perhaps many people speak ill of their neighbours for no other reason, than that they have nothing else to say. Keep your heart with all diligence, to prevent the rise of those evil passions, such as pride, envy, resentment, avarice, ill-nature, and idle curiosity, which commonly lead to evil-speaking. Lastly, set a constant guard over your lips, that ye may not speak unadvisedly, rashly, uncharitably. Deliberately form, and firmly adhere to David's resolution, "I said I will take heed to my ways, that I sin not with my tongue."

On Induſtry.

Rom. xii. 11.

Not ſlothful in buſineſs.

The whole ſtructure of our nature, and the whole condition of our being, proves, that our Maker intended us not for a life of indolence, but of active exertion. All the organs of the body and all the faculties of the mind are inſtruments of action, and are to be employed in the vigorous purſuit of happineſs. It is only by conſtant exerciſe that theſe powers can be preſerved in a ſound and healthful ſtate. If the body be ſuffered to remain long inactive, it will loſe its ſtrength,

strength, and become a prey to disease; at the same time the mental faculties will be gradually enfeebled, and the whole fabric of human happiness be undermined by fretfulness and spleen. It is, on the contrary, a matter of constant experience, that a regular course of bodily exercise is conducive to health, exhilarates the spirits, and contributes to the easy and successful employment of the intellectual powers. The frequent application of the mind to study establishes a habit of thinking, which renders it easy and pleasant to engage in any kind of scientific or literary pursuit: whereas a mind which remains long unemployed loses its delicacy and vigour, and sinks into languor and stupidity. As the earth, if it be industriously cultivated, will produce fruits in rich abundance, but if it be suffered to lie long untilled it will be overrun with weeds, which will be rank in proportion to the richness of the soil; so the human mind,

mind, if cultivated with great affiduity, will yield a plentiful harveft of knowledge and wifdom ; but if it be neglected, it will foon be overfpread with the weeds of error and folly; and thefe poifonous weeds will fpring up in the greateft abundance in thofe minds which are by nature capable of producing the moft excellent fruits. To a mind thus corrupted by indolence the words of Solomon may be applied : " I went by the field of the flothful, and by the vineyard of the man void of underftanding, and lo, it was all grown over with thorns, and nettles had covered the face thereof." The unqueftionable truth is, that man is made for action; and his faculties, like metallic inftruments, if they be not polifhed with ufing, will be confumed by the ruft of indolence.

It is a proof of the goodnefs of our Creator, that he has connected an immediate pleafure with every natural and moderate

moderate exertion of our powers. This is so certain, that there is no definition of the term enjoyment, which is more comprehensive and perfect than that which describes it as consisting in such a moderate exercise and agitation of the mind as, without producing any sensation of fatigue, relieves it from the languor and listlessness of inaction. It would be impossible perhaps to devise any punishment more severe than that of perpetual solitude without employment. The mind which is unoccupied upon external objects must, like a stomach destitute of food, prey upon itself. Every one who wishes to be happy must go out of himself by keeping his mind continually busy in some interesting labour or pursuit. In this sense the maxim is true, that " no man liveth to himself."

But besides the immediate pleasure which attends action as such, there is a certain vigour and alacrity of mind, accompanying

companying habitual induſtry, which prepares it to encounter every difficulty with cheerfulneſs, and which renders every burden light. Diligence inſpires a man with reſolution and fortitude in the execution of every important purpoſe; and renders thoſe labours eaſy and pleaſant which to the ſlothful man would appear irkſome and almoſt inſupportable. An indolent temper leads a man to magnify real difficulties into impoſſibilities, and to diſhearten himſelf by creating a thouſand imaginary obſtacles. The ſlothful man ſaith, "there is a lion in the way, there is a lion in the ſtreets;" he either believes, or pretends to believe, that the path of his duty is beſet with dangers, and therefore excuſes himſelf from purſuing it. The conſequence is, that he is a ſtranger to that ſelf-complacency which ever attends a conſciouſneſs of being well employed. To be able in the midſt of labour and fatigue to reflect, that we are spending our time in a manner which will bear the review, that neither our own hearts, nor our families, nor our country, nor our Maker, can reproach us with having wasted our time in sloth, or in frivolous and unprofitable pursuits, must be a source of unspeakable satisfaction. And since in all labour there is profit, the prospect of reaping the fruits of our industry will not fail to alleviate the burden of daily labour. Why does the husbandman cheerfully endure the fatigues of the field, the sailor encounter the dangers of the sea, or the scholar prosecute his studies with invincible perseverance, but because each expects to reap the respective fruits of his labours, wealth and plenty, or knowledge and wisdom? Hope continually waits upon industry, and points to some distant reward, by which she will at length be amply repaid.

And the rewards of industry are as numerous

merous as the bleffings of Divine Providence. For such is the wife conftitution of the world in which we live, that nothing valuable is to be obtained without induftry. Our Maker has furrounded us with the fources and means of enjoyment, and furnifhed us with powers for purfuing and attaining the objects of our defires: but to afford an agreeable exercife for our faculties, and to give us the pleafing confcioufnefs of being inftruments and agents in the hands of Divine Providence, for our own happinefs and that of our brethren, he hath wifely ordained, that the actual poffeffion of good fhould in a great meafure depend upon our own exertions. Hence it is that the bleffings which we are taught to fupplicate in our prayers, we are alfo required to ufe every lawful means of obtaining. We mock God by our devotions if we afk bleffings which we take no pains to procure. It is a juft obfervation of an ancient writer, that "we ought only to expect prosperity as the fruit of industry and prudence; if we abandon ourselves to sloth, we supplicate the Deity in vain, for he is angry with us." For this reason, too, it is our duty to be thankful to God for those enjoyments which are immediately the fruits of our own industry: his good providence hath established such a connexion between labour and profit, that it is a matter of common and almost universal experience, that success is the reward of industry. It may be admitted as a general maxim, liable only to a few exceptions, for which it would not be difficult in each particular case to assign the reason, that "the soul of the sluggard desireth and hath nothing, but the hand of the diligent maketh rich."

This rule may be applied with equal propriety to every object of human pursuit.

Plentiful supplies of the natural produce

duce of the ground, though the gift of him who visiteth the earth and watereth it, whose clouds drop fatness, and who crowneth the year with his goodness, are also the rewards of human industry. "He that tilleth his land shall be satisfied with bread; but the sluggard shall beg in harvest, and have nothing: the idle shall suffer hunger."

Riches, which are sought with so much avidity by mankind in general, as the means of relieving them from the burden of labour, and of gratifying all their desires, can be honestly acquired in no other method than a diligent application to business: and honest industry is so far crowned with the blessings of heaven, that it seldom fails of acquiring that competency which with a contented mind is true riches. Although it be undoubtedly true, that it is the Lord who giveth power to get wealth, it is not less true, that " he who gathereth by labour shall increase." " Seest thou a man diligent in business,"

faith

faith Solomon, " he shall stand before kings; he shall not stand before mean men." On the other hand, it is a certain truth, confirmed by innumerable facts, that slothfulness is the parent of poverty. " Go to the ant, thou sluggard: consider her ways, and be wise; which having no guide, overseer, or ruler, provideth her meat in the summer, and gathereth her food in the harvest. How long wilt thou sleep, O sluggard? when wilt thou arise out of thy sleep? Yet a little sleep, a little slumber, a little folding of the hands to sleep: so shall thy poverty come as one that travelleth, and thy wants as an armed man."—" Drowsiness shall clothe a man with rags." The wise man adds— " He that is slothful in his work is brother to him that is a great waster:" that is, want of industry in business will no less expose a man to poverty than prodigality itself.

Is the ruling object of your desire and ambition, reputation or fame? this too must

must be the fruit of industry. It is only by a diligent cultivation of the powers of reason, imagination, and memory, that those accomplishments can be acquired which are the foundation of literary fame. It is only by prosecuting important and useful designs with assiduity and perseverance, that a man can distinguish himself among his fellow-citizens as a useful member of society. The man who engages in any laudable enterprize with ardour, and pursues his end with cool and steady resolution, will seldom fail of obtaining that applause which always attends success. Industry is the sure road to advancement; for it qualifies a man for whatever he undertakes, and creates a general partiality in his favour. No industrious man, however mean his station in life may be, provided his conduct be in other respects free from vice, can be contemptible. Neglect and contempt are, indeed, the certain portion of the slothful man. Having neither the
spirit

spirit to undertake, nor the resolution to execute, any laudable design, he lives in obscurity and oblivion; and when he dies he is forgotten as if he had never been. "He that sleepeth in harvest is a son that causeth shame." But the man who "eateth not the bread of idleness," discovers a generous spirit which disdains to subsist, like the drone, upon the provision which has been gathered by the labour of others, and is ambitious of contributing his part towards the general stock; he therefore cannot fail of obtaining the esteem and applause of those who partake of the fruits of his labours.

Does any one direct his ambition towards those intellectual and moral attainments which constitute the wealth of the mind, knowledge, wisdom, and virtue? Industry is no less necessary in this case than in the former. Scientific knowledge of every kind must be acquired by attentive observation and patient thinking. To discover the truth through all the mists

mists of error in which it is involved; to disentangle the intricate web of sophistry; to rise superior to the enslaving influence of authority; to weigh opinions in the even balance of reason; to observe the dependence of truths upon each other, and, after a diligent comparison of discordant tenets, to frame a clear and connected system of principles; to try all things, and at last hold fast that which is true, is an undertaking of great labour and difficulty. To take up opinions upon the credit of others, indolently to repose our judgment upon their authority, is easy enough; but to judge for ourselves requires close attention and unwearied application. A man may, without much difficulty, acquire a power of talking fluently and deciding peremptorily; but he will not find it so easy a task to reason accurately and impartially. Real knowledge is a rich treasure which idleness is unable to purchase. A slothful man may be conceited, but he can never be truly wise.

wife. " A fluggard, " faith the author of the book of Proverbs, " is wifer in his own conceit than feven men that can render a reafon."

Practical wifdom, or the knowledge of the effential principles and fundamental laws of religion and virtue, is an attainment attended with lefs difficulty; but even this cannot be gained without a diligent ftudy of the human heart, a careful obfervation of human life, and a ferious attention to the doctrine of the holy Scriptures, which are able to make men wife unto falvation. It is in the perfon of wifdom that Solomon fays—" Bleffed is the man that heareth me watching daily at my gates, waiting at the pofts of my doors: for whofo findeth me findeth life, and fhall obtain favour of the Lord."

The application of the maxims and precepts of wifdom in the conduct of life, or the practice of virtue, alfo requires conftant attention and unwearied diligence. How much neceffity there is for induftry in this moſt important affair, will be evident to every one who attends to the variety and extent of human duty, and to the numerous obſtacles which lie in the path of obedience. To root out pernicious prejudices; to correct vicious habits; to curb irregular appetites; to reſiſt powerful temptations; to diſcharge with fidelity our various obligations to God and man; to perform religious duties with uninterrupted attention, and with a ſerious and hearty aſſent to every verbal expreſſion of devotion; to maintain an habitual regard to the providence and authority of God through every ſcene of life; to preſerve an inflexible regard to integrity and honeſty, in oppoſition to all the enticements of avarice and ambition; in a word, to be ſteadily and uniformly virtuous in the midſt of evil examples; to do all this, muſt require conſtant attention, vigilant circumſpection, and perſevering induſtry. And yet all this is abſolutely neceſſary, if we wiſh to accompliſh

complish that great point which ought to be the ultimate end of all our wishes and pursuits, the attainment of eternal happiness. " Everlasting life is indeed the gift of God through Jesus Christ our Lord;" but it is also the appointed reward of a patient continuance in well-doing; and they who wish to obtain this glorious prize, must " run with patience the race set before them."

It must be added here, that not only is industry necessary to the attainment of virtue, as well as every other valuable accomplishment and possession, but it is in its own nature, even when employed in the ordinary occupations and pursuits of life, an important guard to virtue, and a good security against temptation. Whilst the mind is seriously intent upon important business it is already too much occupied to leave room for the intrusion of evil thoughts and designs. The indolent man, on the contrary, lies open to every assault of temptation, and is prepared to

listen

listen to any proposal which may relieve him from the burden of reflection, and rouse his torpid faculties into action. A state of inactivity is so unnatural to man, that to free themselves from it men will condescend to commit any folly, and almost any vice. It was when David was loitering at home, instead of attending his army in person, as he had been accustomed to do, that he fell into that destructive snare which involved him in complicated guilt, laid the foundation of bitter remorse, and fixed a blot upon his character and memory which will never be effaced. It is recorded in scripture, that in that city which was so abandoned to wickedness that God sent fire from heaven to destroy it, one of its prevailing characters was idleness. " Behold, this was the iniquity of Sodom, pride, fulness of bread, and abundance of idleness was in her." It is a memorable fact in the history of ancient Rome, which illustrates and confirms our present observation, that

when

when that ardent spirit of liberty which had kept the people in a state of perpetual agitation during the period of the republic, was suppressed, and a dead calm was spread over the city by the tyranny of imperial government; and when their extensive conquests furnished ample supplies of luxury, without the help of labour or commerce; they sunk down into a degree of contemptible effeminacy and gross depravity not to be paralleled in any other period of the history of Europe. From these and other similar facts it may be concluded with certainty, that habitual indolence produces dissoluteness of manners. One fault into which persons of an indolent temper are in danger of falling may deserve to be particularly mentioned; I mean that with which the apostle Paul charged some of his brethren in Thessalonica—" They learn to be idle, wandering about from house to house; and not only idle, but tatlers also, and busy bodies, speaking things which they

ought

ought not." It is a common thing for those who neglect their own affairs, to fill up the heavy hours of their indolent existence with prying into the affairs of others; extorting and communicating secrets; impertinently meddling with business which does not concern them; circulating, and perhaps inventing, idle and slanderous tales, which can serve no other possible end than to injure respectable characters, and disturb the peace of happy families:—a character so contemptible, as well as mischievous, that a wise man will occupy his leisure with any innocent employment or amusement, rather than subject himself by *indolence* to the temptation of becoming a *busy-body.*

I will only add one farther consideration to recommend a life of virtuous industry, which is, that it is an inexhaustible source of pleasing reflections, both whilst it is passing and when it is closed. In the small intervals of rest from the more arduous and important business of life, the industrious man will partake of its comforts and amusements with a pleasure of which the indolent can form no conception. A consciousness that he is endeavouring to discharge with all diligence the duties of life, will render his refreshments grateful, his recreations enlivening, and his repose pleasant. Even "the sleep of the labouring man is sweet." Not a single evening arrives which brings with it the gloomy reflection, "I have lost a day:" and when the days of his labour are all ended, the man who has passed his life in honest industry finds that he has been storing up in his memory and conscience a rich and inexhaustible fund of consolation. He can review with complacency the prosperity of his circumstances, the happy state of his family, the intellectual furniture of his mind, and the virtues of his character, as monuments of his industry. In this sense it is true, that the substance of a diligent man is precious. What he has acquired by the

labour

labour of his hands he highly prizes, and enjoys with delight; and when he is called by the providence of God to resign to his heirs the fruits of his earthly labours, if he has at the same time given all diligence, by the practice of virtue, to lay up treasures in heaven, he can look forwards to an incorruptible inheritance beyond the grave, well persuaded that " to him that soweth righteousness there shall be a sure reward." In this important sense the maxim is true—" Cast thy bread upon the waters, and thou shalt find it again after many days."

The practical use which we should make of this discourse is, to learn to look upon the labours of life, not as a burden, but a pleasure; and to perform our respective tasks, whether of secular business, intellectual improvement, moral action, or religious duty, with diligence and alacrity. Since we are fixed in our respective stations by the great Lord of nature, and have our proper business allotted us, for our own benefit and that of our brethren; whatsoever our hands find to do, let us do it with all our might; saying, after the example of Christ—" I must work the work of him that sent me whilst it is day; for the night cometh, wherein no man can work."

Caution in forming, and Constancy in preserving, Friendships re-recommended.

PROVERBS xxvii. 10.

Thine own friend, and thy father's friend, forsake not.

THERE is not a more pleasing topic of declamation, or a topic which hath more frequently employed the pens of philosophers and moralists, than friendship. We often read of its mighty power to enliven and cheer the heart of man, to heighten his pleasures and alleviate his sorrows, and to make his days, whether they be fair or foul, pass smoothly and pleasantly along.

How far the actual experience of mankind agrees with the pictures which have been

been drawn by poets and philosophers in their closets, it may perhaps be difficult to determine. There are doubtless social, benevolent, and tender feelings, in the human heart; there is, doubtless, in nature such a thing as friendship: and, possibly, those who are possessed of an uncommon share of natural sensibility, cultivated and strengthened by a liberal and refined education, and who have had the happiness to form connexions with persons whose sentiments and tastes are similar to their own, may see reason to think that the union of hearts which subsists between intimate friends is productive of pleasures little inferior to any thing which the poet's pen can describe, or his fancy conceive. Possibly, with such persons, friendship is so dear and sacred a name, that, at the bare mention of it, " their hearts burn within them."

But when young persons enter into life with too exalted notions of friendship and benevolence, and too high expectations from

from mankind, (which their own warm and generous difpofitions, and the ufual ſtrain of the books they read, concur to give them) it frequently happens, that, after a few difappointments, they find themfelves obliged to lower their opinion of human life, and begin to think that they have hitherto only amufed themfelves with romantic dreams, and that pure, difinterefted, immutable friendfhip, is little better than an agreeable fiction, the creature of a gay and youthful fancy : and it is well if the mortification and pain which attend this difcovery do not four their tempers, make them diffatisfied with the world, and indifpofe them for enjoying even the real pleafures of focial life.

It is not, however, folely to be afcribed to the imperfection of human nature, or to the flattering ideas which we are apt at firſt to entertain concerning the world, that we meet with fuch frequent difappointments, and fo feldom enjoy, in any degree of perfection, the pleasures of friendship. There are other causes that concur to produce this effect which lie much more within our own power, and to which, for the sake of our own peace, we should pay particular attention. One of the principal of these is, that we are not sufficiently sensible of the value of an old and approved friend, and are too apt, on slight grounds, to reject and forsake him, and to receive others into our hearts before we can have had sufficient proof that they are worthy of such confidence.

What is present with us, and we call our own, we are too apt to despise and undervalue. What is at a distance, and not yet at our command, we usually prize at too high a rate. Possession diminishes, expectation and desire magnify, the worth of every object which comes under our notice. Thus it is with regard to friendship. The friends we have already gained, whose fidelity we have tried, and whose affection we have experienced, we are

are too apt to disregard and treat with indifference, at the very time when we ought to receive them to our bosoms with the most cordial affection—when their sincerity has been sufficiently tried, and fully approved. When the charm of novelty is over, it requires no common share of good sense, and steadiness of temper, to preserve that uniform and inviolable attachment, without which friendship is but a name. The first ardours of affection are generally too violent to continue; and it is often seen that they gradually subside into indifference, and are even changed into contempt and hatred. These disagreeable revolutions in friendships frequently happen amongst young persons, between whom we rarely find that calm and steady attachment which is founded in judgment and established by experience. Various reasons may be assigned to account for this fact.

There is in most young persons a certain restlessness and unsteadiness of temper, which prevents them from dwelling long upon any one particular object, and inclines them to wander from flower to flower in search of new sweets. Such is their love of novelty and variety, that, for the sake of the pleasure of forming a new acquaintance, they will too often treat an old one with neglect, and cast him aside as an old garment which is no longer fit for use; as if they thought that their friendships, like their clothes, must of course decay with time, or were made of such frail materials that they must at last be worn out. Nay, we sometimes see them discovering the same humour and caprice with respect to their attachments as they do with respect to dress, and changing both for no better reason than that they are tired of them and wish for something new.

Another cause of the inconstancy of youthful friendships is, that young persons, having formed exalted ideas of friendship, entertained a good opinion of mankind,

kind, and had but little experience of their weakness and inconstancy, are ready to expect, in those they make choice of as their intimate associates, every thing that is amiable and excellent, without any disagreeable alloy. The consequence of which is, that when, upon a thorough acquaintance and frequent intercourse, they discover certain foibles which they did not expect, they are apt to imagine that they have been deceived in their choice, and to reject a friend as unworthy of their esteem and confidence, for no other reason but because he is not—what a little knowledge of the world will soon convince him that no man is—a perfect character. A small degree of vehemence of temper— a slight instance of imprudence or inattention—one rash word or action which arose from no corrupt principle— shall be considered as a sufficient reason for rejecting, with indignation and contempt, a judicious, faithful, and affectionate friend. Whereas observation and
experience

experience would have taught them, that such a friend is a treasure too scarce and too valuable to be thrown away upon every slight pretence; and that he who wishes to have a friend, must learn to " bear a friend's infirmities."

It may be assigned as another reason why young persons are apt to be fickle in their friendships, that as their minds gradually open, and they increase in knowledge and experience, their opinions, taste, and manners, are continually liable to variation. A youthful mind is like a tender plant, which may be bent in one direction or in another, and is capable of receiving different forms at pleasure, before it is grown to its full maturity. It is not till we are pretty far advanced in life that our views of things, and our habits of action, are fixed and determined. Before this is done, we generally pass through several revolutions in our opinions, our dispositions, and our characters. It is not therefore at all surprising, that a young person,

person, when he first enters into social attachments, should think that man possessed of all the qualities which he wishes to find in a friend, whom afterwards he may not be able, merely through a change in his own ideas and sentiments, and not through any fault in his friend, to treat with the same freedom and affection as formerly. Some cases of this kind may occur, in which an intimacy shall gradually die away without any material fault, and without any direct design, in either party. There are, however, other cases, in which valuable friendships are given up, and a mutual alienation takes place, in consequence of a change of opinion on subjects in which friendship has no immediate concern, and not unfrequently in consequence of an accidental change in situation or fortune. But on these, or any other slight grounds, to dissolve the sacred band of friendship, is not only to betray a culpable fickleness of temper, but to be lavish of treasures which cannot be easily regained.

Numerous are the advantages which may be derived from friendship. A true friend will instruct and advise you in circumstances of difficulty; he will enliven your social hours with free and cheerful conversation; he will minister consolation to your hearts in the time of distress; and he will always be ready to lend you assistance to the utmost of his power. Various and important are the qualifications which are necessary to form the character of a faithful and useful friend:— a generous and liberal turn of mind, a tender and affectionate heart, a good understanding, prudence and discretion, and, above all, a soul superior to mean and sordid views, and capable of interesting itself warmly in the happiness of another. Seldom can we expect to find all these qualifications united in one person. If, therefore, we have met with a friend who possesses them in any considerable degree, we should rejoice in our good fortune, and prize him as the " immediate jewel of of our foul." It is the advice of the fon of Sirach—" Change not a friend for any good, neither a faithful friend for the gold of Ophir."

And yet, notwithftanding the ineftimable value of a *true friend*, notwithftanding every one acknowledges that fuch a friend is rarely to be found, how often do we fee young perfons neglecting thofe who after trial bid faireft to deferve this character, and receiving to their bofoms every new candidate for their affections who falls in their way? If a young perfon be poffeffed of a tolerable fhare of underftanding, and a polite and engaging addrefs, and efpecially if he have any pretenfions to wit and humour, and difcover that difpofition towards experice which is generally confidered as a mark of an open and generous fpirit; without hefitation or referve, they court his friendfhip, lay open before him the fecrets of their hearts, pay an implicit deference to his opinions, and fuffer him to mould their difpofiticns and characters

at

at his pleasure: when probably a little prudent precaution and delay might have convinced them that, notwithstanding all his shining attractions, and all his real accomplishments, he is an ensnaring and dangerous companion, instead of being an agreeable and faithful friend.

I dwell the longer and with the greater earnestness upon this subject, because it is by this precipitate and unthinking manner of forming friendships that so many young persons are led into practices which they in their hearts disapprove, and acquire habits of irrregularity and vice before they are aware. I would not encourage a suspicious temper. I wish every one to think as well of mankind as the real state of things will permit: but, after all, it is a matter of great importance, that young persons should be convinced, if possible, by other means than their own experience, that it is not every man who is capable of being a true friend—that under the appearance of much good-nature, civilvility, and politeness, may lie concealed a bad heart—and that "all is not gold which glitters."

The establishment of friendships—I speak more particularly to young persons—you ought to consider as a very serious business. A judicious, affectionate, and faithful friend, may prove the greatest blessing of life; but a treacherous, a vicious, or even an imprudent friend, may be the means of your utter ruin.

It is only from long observation of the abilities, dispositions, and character of a man, and from repeated trials of his integrity and generosity in smaller instances, that you can judge whether he is qualified to be a friend: and it is at least as probable, that you will suffer inconvenience, as that you will reap advantage, from every attachment which is formed without mature deliberation, and a thorough knowledge of the man whom you admit to your bosom. A stranger may be able to entertain or improve you by his conversation; he may agree with you in opinion and sentiment; he may shew you much civility; he may do you real service; and yet, after all, there may be something in his temper or character which would make it highly imprudent in you to choose him for your friend. Whilst you only consider him as a general acquaintance, occasionally associate with him, and interchange the common offices of politeness and civility, you have no right to suppose that there are any such defects in his character; but, before you take him to your heart, you ought to be very certain that *there are not*. "If thou wouldest get a friend, prove him first, and be not hasty to credit him. For some man is a friend for his own occasion, and will not abide in the day of thy trouble; and there is a friend, who being turned to enmity and reproach, will discover thy reproach." Again—" Some friend is a companion at the table, and will not continue in the day of thy affliction. In thy prosperity

prosperity he will be as thyself, and will be bold over thy servants; but if thou be brought low, he will be against thee, and will hide himself from thy face."

The sum of what hath been said is, that you should be cautious and deliberate in forming, and steady and determined in preserving friendships. You should not wish to contract an intimacy with every one who upon a slight acquaintance appears to be agreeable, or consider every man as worthy a place in your hearts, who is capable of entertaining or improving you by his conversation, or " who is wont to set the table in a roar;" for the most learned men, or the greatest wits, are not always the best friends.

You should make choice of such for your intimate companions as appear, upon careful examination, to be possessed of a good understanding and useful knowledge without pedantry; to be prudent without artifice; and to be kind and generous from the natural goodness of their hearts, without pride or affectation: and having found such friends, you should bind them to your hearts with "cords of love," and suffer nothing but death to dissolve the union which reason, prudence, benevolence and virtue, have formed. "Forsake not an old friend, for the new is not comparable to him; a new friend is like new wine, when it is old thou shalt drink it with pleasure."— " Thine own friend, and thy father's friend, forsake not."

At the same time, however, that you are assiduous to secure and to perpetuate the blessings of friendship, be careful to deserve them. Never forget, that " he that hath a friend, must shew himself friendly." Between minds, as well as between bodies, attraction can subsist no longer than it is reciprocal; and mutual kindness can only be cherished by mutual endeavours to serve and oblige. If you are frequently receiving from your friend tokens of attachment and affection, watch

for

for opportunities of making equivalent returns; or if inequality of condition should on your part render this impracticable, be the more careful to seize every occasion of expressing, in ways not inconsistent with the delicacy of friendship, your sense of obligation. Above all, study to render yourself worthy of the friendship you value, by cherishing all those amiable qualities, and practising all those substantial virtues, which unite to form the character of a true friend. More particularly cultivate the kind and generous affections. " Friendship is the reciprocation of affection; and he who has none to bestow, has no right to expect any in return." To hope to gain a friend without this, is as if the merchant should expect to purchase a jewel of the highest value without being able or willing to pay the price for it. On the contrary, kindness will always be found to produce kindness; and no man will fail to be rich in the returns of love, who is careful to

purchase

purchase it with the payment of love. Exercise an habitual command over yourselves, to check those sudden gusts of ill-humour or passion which the casual interference of opinions, inclinations, or interests, may tend to excite. The maxim is well-founded, that friendship is not to be formed with an angry man. Be ever ready to allow to your friend that indulgence which you claim for yourself; and rather by gentleness and forbearance invite generosity, than by a rude and unyielding assertion of your right awaken the latent spirit of discord. Be upon your guard against every propensity towards *peevishness* and *fretfulness*. Nothing is more dissonant to the tones of love than the harsh murmurs of discontent. Friendship loves to breathe a free and pleasant air, and to bask in the sunshine of cheerfulness; amidst the fogs and damps of fretfulness, it sickens and dies. Even in sorrow, if you wish to secure the consolations of friendship, you must refrain from

from peevish and ill-humoured complaints. Friendship must provide itself against the storm as well as the calm; and he who wishes to preserve a friend to the last hour of his life, must endeavour to carry a mild, placid, and affectionate temper, through all the vicissitudes of the world. Cherish that *generosity* of spirit which will enable you easily and cheerfully to part with the gifts of fortune at the call of friendship. Live in the constant habit of participating and communicating with all around you, and with those most who are most deserving of your affection. Finally, let your friendships be cemented and perpetuated by *virtue*. A friendly heart is the united result of all the virtues; and it is exactly in the proportion in which virtuous dispositions and manners are cultivated, that we are prepared to discharge the duties and enjoy the pleasures of friendship in this life, and to participate in the social felicities of the life to come.

Prayer for a Competency.

Proverbs xxx. 8.

Feed me with food convenient for me.

It is one of the moſt important leſſons which true wiſdom and which religion teacheth, that we ſhould apply our principal attention to the culture of our minds, and the acquiſition of thoſe poſſeſſions which are of a moral and ſpiritual nature. If we deſire to be happy either in this world, or that which is to come, it ſhould be our chief care, not to increaſe in riches, and riſe in power, but to improve ourſelves in the habits of piety, benevolence, humility, contentment and fortitude,

fortitude, and in every other virtue. This will give us the true enjoyment of life, under all the viciffitudes of fortune; this will qualify us for our entrance into a future ftate, and enable us to be happy in a world where thofe objects, which at prefent fo much engage our attention, will be no longer within our reach. It muft, however, be granted, that whilft we are in this world, it is natural that we fhould pay fome degree of regard to its interefts, nay, that it is impoffible for us wholly to neglect them. Nature will always prompt us to defire and purfue thofe things which are neceffary for the fupport of life, and even thofe things which are requifite and ufeful to render our prefent exiftence eafy and comfortable: whilft life itfelf is an object of defire, we muft feek thofe things which will contribute to its prefervation and happinefs. And it can never be unreafonable to give thefe objects a confiderable

fhare

share of attention in the course of our lives, and even to allow them a place in our devotion. Accordingly we find, that our Saviour himself, though he constantly inculcated the greatest moderation and self-denial upon his disciples, nevertheless permitted them to follow the dictates of nature, in desiring and praying for those things which are necessary for the support and comforts of life. In that form of prayer which he taught them, he thought it not improper to insert a petition which relates entirely to the things of this world, " give us this day our daily bread." The prayer of Agur in the text, " Feed me with food convenient for me," is, then, a petition which may reasonably find a place in our devotions. To explain its true meaning, and unfold the sentiments which it expresses, will be the business of this discourse.

In the first place, when we pray to the Almighty, that he would feed us with

with food convenient for us, we express a humble sense of our dependence upon God, for all the necessary supports and conveniencies of life. We acknowledge that we must be indebted to a higher power than our own, for the bread which we eat, and the raiment with which we are clothed, and for every thing which we enjoy. We declare our humble conviction of the insufficiency of all our most prudent and industrious efforts to furnish ourselves with these things, without the Divine concurrence and blessing. We express our firm persuasion that, " except the Lord build the house, they labour in vain that build it," and that whatever secondary means or instruments may contribute to our support and happiness, we ought to look beyond these to the Great First Cause and Director of all, and ascribe every good thing we enjoy to his wise and merciful providence. And what sentiment, my brethren, can be

more

more rational or becoming than this? The frame of human nature, and every object in the world around us, affords us the most convincing proofs of Almighty power, of wise design, and of perfect benevolence.

Now, from this fundamental and evident truth, it immediately follows, that all creatures depend entirely upon the providence of God for every circumstance of their being. That we are capable of receiving nourishment and pleasure from the fruits of the earth, is to be ascribed to that wisdom and goodness which gives us organs suited to the several functions of animal life. That these organs daily receive their proper supplies is, because the Almighty continually preserveth the course of nature which his wisdom and goodness had established, and giveth us fruitful times and seasons. That we have not only the necessary supports of life, but a variety of gratifications suited to our several

several senses, is owing to the bounty of our heavenly father, who openeth his hand and satisfieth the desire of every living thing, and who giveth us all things richly to enjoy. Our daily bread, and many of the comforts of life, may indeed be the fruit of our own industry and skill, or the liberality of others. It is agreeable to the established course of things, that our own exertions should be necessary in procuring the common supports of life. And we are frequently indebted to the kindness and generosity of our friends for those things which neither our own industry nor skill could have obtained. But whence is it that we derive that strength of body or those powers of mind which qualify us for filling up some useful station in life, and hereby procuring a decent competence for ourselves or families? Whence is it that our friends and benefactors derive all their ability and inclination to assist us; and who is it that hath

given

given to some that abundance of the good things of life, which enables them to minister to the necessities of their brethren, and hath inspired them with humane and friendly affections? All these capacities and enjoyments proceed from that Being who giveth to all creatures life and breath, and all things; and therefore we are as much dependent upon the Almighty for those blessings which we receive through the instrumentality of our own labours, or the generosity of others, as if they were bestowed upon us by an immediate and miraculous interposition of Divine Providence. Since the truth of all this is manifest beyond contradiction, can any thing be more becoming than that we should maintain a continual sense of our dependence upon the Almighty for all our supports and enjoyments, and that we should frequently express this in solemn acts of worship? Such exercises as these will naturally increase creafe that pious regard to the Supreme Being in all the events of our lives, which fo well becomes creatures who are continually dependent upon and infinitely indebted to their Creator. If we frequently acknowledge our ftate of dependence, we fhall daily become more humble and thankful; more humble under a fenfe of our own weaknefs and indigence; and more thankful for the continual care and bleffing of heaven. And we fhall hereby be induced to make a religious and careful improvement of the bounties of Divine Providence. Inftead of making them fubfervient to the gratification of irregular and inordinate paffions, we fhould learn to ufe them with moderation and for the benefit of our fellow-creatures, that we may be able to give a good account of ourfelves, and of the talents committed unto us, to the great Lord of all. Such is the reafonablenefs and importance of expreffing a humble fenfe of

our

our dependence upon Divine Providence in the words of the text, " feed me with food convenient for me."

When we adopt this language, we likewise express our earnest desire and humble hope, that the Almighty will grant unto us a competent share of the good things of this life. We look up unto him, as unto the father of the family of the whole earth, who provideth a plentiful and suitable support for all his offspring, and spreadeth a table before them richly stored with every thing needful for their preservation and comfort, as part of this happy family. We express a natural desire that we may partake of the abundant provision which he hath made, as well as our brethren, and a cheerful confidence in his impartial goodness, that he will not neglect or despise our prayer, but will treat us with his wonted goodness and liberality, and bestow upon us whatever he shall see to be good

good for us. We are not indeed to look up unto him for the supply of our wants, while we neglect the proper and diligent use of those means with which he hath furnished us for this purpose. It is the manifest design of the Almighty to convey the blessings of his providence unto us through the channel of our own industry and prudence. The bread which we eat doth not grow spontaneously from the earth, but is to be prepared and provided for our use by a long course of labour and attention. Nothing could be more absurd or profane than for a man to leave his lands uncultivated, and neglect the accustomed methods of providing for a plentiful harvest, and when he finds that he is disappointed of his usual crop, to pray that God would feed him with food convenient for him. And in every other instance we find that, according to the general course of things, the only way to gain the objects of our desire is to employ ourselves, with industry, in the pursuit of them. But as this is no objection against the reasonableness of prayer, since all our success and happiness depend upon the divine blessing; so neither do we want sufficient encouragement for prayer while we accompany our devotions with a diligent use of the means which Heaven hath appointed for the attainment of those things for which we pray. Have we not continually experienced the care of Divine Providence in our past lives? Hath not every day been crowned with new mercies, and given us fresh proofs that the Lord is good to all, and that his tender mercies are over all his works? Have we not received the bread of every day in its season? Has there been a single day in which the good Father of all hath failed to provide for us, or forgotten to be gracious unto us? Even when we have neglected to supplicate his protection and blessing, or to acknowledge

knowledge his mercies, hath he not paſſed by our ingratitude, and ſtill continued to do us good? Why then ſhould we entertain a doubt that he will lend a merciful ear to the voice of our ſupplication, and grant unto us thoſe ſupplies, from the inexhauſtible ſtores of his bounty, which he ſhall ſee to be beſt for us? Surely we ought with the greateſt cheerfulneſs to look up unto him, who hath hitherto been our liberal benefactor and our beſt friend, for the ſupply of our future wants; and may ſecurely rely upon his goodneſs, that while we truſt in him, and obey him, we ſhall want no good thing. "Truſt in the Lord and do good, and verily thou ſhalt be fed." But I proceed to obſerve,

That when we make uſe of the language of the text in our prayer, we do likewiſe hereby expreſs the moderation of our deſires with regard to the things of this life. In praying with Agur, "feed me with food convenient for me," we only pray unto our Heavenly Father for those things which are necessary for our support and preservation. The sentiments we express are such as these: If thou, the wise dispenser of good, shalt see fit to give us abundance, we will thankfully receive and enjoy it, as the gift of thy bounty; but we are persuaded that our happiness doth not consist in the abundance of the things which we possess; directing our desires and pursuits principally towards the riches of the mind, we will cheerfully acquiesce in thine appointments with respect to our external condition in life, whatsoever it may be, and only pray that thou wouldest give us our portion of meat in due season. That such sentiments as these are perfectly agreeable to the principles of true wisdom and genuine piety, every one who examines the nature and condition of man, and reflects upon the perfections and providence of God, must be convinced.

Though

Though riches are generally purfued with the greateft eagernefs, as if they were the certain and only means of happinefs; though it be lawful to receive and enjoy them within the limitations which honefty and humanity prefcribe, when they offer themfelves to our acceptance; and though, under the direction of wifdom, benevolence, and piety, they may be rendered fubfervient to the moft valuable purpofes, it needs no laboured arguments to prove that they are not effential to human felicity. The world furnifhes us with innumerable inftances of perfons who poffefs real fatisfactions, and have the true enjoyment of life, who, with the moft diligent labour of their hands, can only procure that fcanty fupport which may with literal propriety be ftyled their daily bread. It will likewife afford inftances, not a few, of thofe who enjoy all the advantages of wealth and power, who are notwithftanding, through the prevalence of spleen and ill-humour, suspicion and jealousy, pride and ambition, revenge and malice, and other turbulent and hateful passions, incapable of real happiness. From all which it is manifest, that true felicity is seated not in external circumstances, but in the temper of the mind; and that the principal object of our wishes and endeavours ought to be, not the increase of our wealth, but the improvement of those virtuous habits of mind which are an eternal source of self-enjoyment. The reasonableness of moderating our desires with regard to riches, and the good things of this life, may likewise be inferred from the consideration of the wise and good providence of God. We see that the Almighty, who ordereth all things with perfect wisdom and goodness, and is the rewarder of all them that seek him, frequently leaves those who are most obedient to his law to struggle with the difficulties of

poverty

povert and diftrefs, while he permits the moft unworthy and profligate of the fons of men to increafe in riches, and, with refpect to external good, to enjoy all that heart can wifh. We may therefore be affured, that he doth not mean to diftinguifh the righteous from the wicked by the gifts of fortune; and this fhould teach us to look upon all thofe enjoyments which are common to good and bad men with comparative indifference, and to make that unwearied felf-approbation, that peace of mind, that joyful perfuafion of the divine favour, and that good hope of everlafting life, which are the peculiar rewards of righteoufnefs, the chief objects of our purfuit. We fhould feek the kingdom of God, and the righteoufnefs thereof, and truft in his good providence, that whatever elfe fhall on the whole be good for us, will be added unto us.

In the laft place, by making ufe of the petition of the text, " feed me with food convenient for me," we declare our cheerful reliance on the protection and care of Providence, with respect to the events of futurity, and disclaim all solicitude and anxiety. Leaving it entirely to the Almighty to determine what that portion of good is, which shall be convenient for us, we banish from our minds all anxious thought with respect to our future condition, assuring ourselves that, whatever it be, it will be that which is on the whole best for us. Now this is a temper of mind for which there is abundant foundation in the principles of religion. If Almighty God directs all events by his unerring wisdom, and disposeth all things in such a manner as most perfectly accomplishes the designs of his goodness, why should we fear any event which may befal us? Have we not all the assurance which the perfection of God can give us, that all things shall work together for good? If any afflictive event should hereafter happen to us, we are instructed to believe,

believe, that it will be no other than the chaſtiſement of a father, deſigned to produce in us the peaceable fruits of righteouſneſs, and to work out for us a far more exceeding and eternal weight of glory. Ought we not then cheerfully to leave the events of futurity in the hands of that Being who hath already dealt ſo bountifully with us, and done ſuch great things for us? What ground can we poſſibly have for painful and diſtreſſing apprehenſions, if we have a witneſs in our own breaſts that we are the objects of the Divine approbation? This teſtimony of our conſciences may inſpire us with a joyful hope, that whatever befals us in this life, our eternal happineſs is ſecure; and that when we have paſſed through the variable and uncertain ſcenes of the preſent world, we ſhall enter on a ſtate of perfect and unchangeable felicity in the kingdom of heaven. And as we have all imaginable encouragement to

baniſh

banish distressing fears and anxious cares from our hearts, it is likewise evident that this is one of the most effectual means of establishing the peace of our minds, and securing our present happiness. The man who is perpetually harassed with distressing apprehensions concerning the future, cannot possibly have any enjoyment of the present; the continual dread of future evils will necessarily destroy his relish for present good: on the other hand, when a man hath left all the events of futurity in the hands in which we should always, and in which we may surely leave them, and hath by this means entirely disengaged himself from the burden of anxiety, how easy and happy must he be in himself, how capable of enjoying the comforts of the present hour with the highest satisfaction, and of alleviating its sorrows and afflictions by peaceful reflections and consolatory hopes! A man who can look up to heaven for the supply of his present wants, without any painful apprehension apprehenfion concerning thofe which are future, is prepared for all the viciffitudes of fortune; he is not afraid of evil bodings, his heart is fixed, trufting in the Lord.—Be it our conftant concern to cultivate this contented, refigned, and happy temper, in obedience to the apoftolic precept—" Be careful for nothing, but in every thing, by prayer and fupplication with thankfgiving, make your requefts known unto God."

Youth

Youth and Age compared.

Psalm xxxvii. 25.

I have been young, and now am old.

This is a confession which men do not easily persuade themselves to make. Old age, like the shades of the evening, steals upon us by imperceptible degrees; and it is not possible to ascertain the exact point at which it commences. Life is commonly divided into four stages, childhood, youth, manhood, and old age. In passing from the first of these to the second, and from the second to the third, we impatiently anticipate the approaching period.

period. Eager to enter upon a new career of enterprize, and upon new scenes of enjoyment, we fancy that we cannot too soon dismiss the badges of childhood, and release ourselves from the restraints of authority, to mingle without controul in the busy and splendid scenes of life. But when the time arrives at which we are to pass into the last period of our present existence, the case is altered. Instead of presenting us with new objects of desire and hope, old age threatens to steal from us the delights we have hitherto possessed, and to leave us in their place an ever-increasing burden of infirmity and disease. We observe with aversion the first approaches of this unwelcome intruder. For a long time we are willing to persuade ourselves that the natural symptoms of declining strength are owing to some accidental cause, which will shortly be removed. If our sight or our hearing begins to lose its wonted quickness; if we perceive some failure of muscular ftrength; if time is furrowing our brow with wrinkles; if "grey hairs are here and there upon us;" we endeavour to forget fuch unpleafant *mementos* of human frailty. Even when accumulated evidence will no longer permit us to doubt that we are growing old, we ftill take pains to hide the painful truth from our own obfervation. And as if it were difgraceful to be thought old; as if the ancient law which enjoins refpect to age were reverfed, we make ufe of every expedient to conceal that length of days which we formerly accounted honourable.

A fmall degree of reflection might be fufficient to correct this weaknefs. Who does not fee that it is the extreme of folly to oppofe the eftablifhed order of things, or to refufe a placid fubmiffion to the immutable laws of nature? Time flows with an irrefiftible current; and, while the world endures, one generation of men will pafs away, and another come. Old age is nothing more than the laft portion

portion of that courfe of exiftence which is allotted to man in this world. It is as natural to us to grow old, and to die, as to be born. To dread the approach of old age, betrays a feeble and ill-inftructed mind. To be afhamed of it, when it arrives, is to caft reproach on the wife allotments of Divine Providence. Our wifdom is to receive the firft intimations of its arrival with tranquillity and firmnefs, and to prepare for all that fhall follow by wife reflections and manly refolutions.

Whatever be the ufual point at which old age commences, it muft be admitted that there is a point in every man's life at which he may firft, with propriety, adopt the words of the text, " I have been *young*, and now am *old.*" This point, wherever it is fixed, may not improperly be confidered as a ftation on the fummit of the hill of human life, from which the traveller may, with the greateft advantage, take a retrofpect of the path over which

which he has already paffed, and a prof-pect of that which yet lies before him; comparing the different, and often contradictory opinions and fentiments of the young and the old, and, on the comparifon, correcting the errors of both, and arriving at a juft and impartial decifion.

From this imagined ftation let us, in the fequel, examine the different judgments of the young and the old on the fubject of *pleafure*; on *riches*; on the CHARACTERS OF MEN; and on the general CONDITION OF HUMAN LIFE.

That the old and the young often differ in opinion and judgment, is a well known fact. This difference is in many cafes fo great as to produce mutual contempt and averfion, and to become the occafion of much domeftic infelicity. The old pity the thoughtleffnefs and folly of the young; the young ridicule the ftupid infenfibility of the old. The fage advice which the aged are fo ready to beftow, as the refult of long experience and obfervation, appears

pears to the young, who view things under a different afpect, to be more frequently the effect of peevifh difcontent than the dictate of wifdom. The wholefome authority which the aged judge it fo neceffary to exercife over the young, in order to reftrain the exceffes of juvenile paffion, is confidered by the objects on which it is exercifed as an infupportable oppreffion. In fhort, the fentiments and taftes of the old and the young are often fo directly oppofite, that, like water and oil, they cannot by any degree of agitation be brought to coalefce.

There is no fubject on which the young and the old entertain fentiments more widely different, than that of *pleafure.* At the very name of pleafure every chord vibrates with delight in the bofom of the young. In whatever form it folicits the fenfes, or entices the imagination, it becomes the object of their idolatry. With affections alive to every impulfe, and fpirits in tune for every joy,

Vol. I. X they

they think it hard not to be permitted to confecrate to pleafure all the golden moments of youth. Serious employment, whenever it interrupts their favourite purfuits, is a grievous burden; and even that ftudy which is neceffary to the acquifition of ufeful knowledge, is a painful drudgery. They are never happy, but when they are mixing in public crowds, where fafhion and vanity prefide, and where admiration is reciprocally excited and beftowed, or when they are revelling in the bowers of voluptuoufnefs, where every fenfe is gratified without the troublefome controul of wifdom.

Very different from thefe are the feelings which fcenes of amufement, gaiety, and pleafure, excite in thofe whofe advanced age oblige them to look backward upon things of this kind as with refpect to themfelves gone paft, never to return. Their experience of the tranfient nature of thefe enjoyments, of the numerous vexations and mortifications which necef-
farily

farily accompany them, and of the serious evils which are the unavoidable consequence of irregular and intemperate indulgence, convince them that their value is much below that which the gay imaginations and eager desires of youth are apt to bestow upon them. And if they made no further use of their superior knowledge, than to inform the young of truths essential to their happiness before they can be taught them by their own experience, instead of deserving censure or contempt, they would be entitled to grateful attention. But we often see the aged passing from the respectable and amiable character of a friendly monitor into that of a rigid and petulant censor. If they have lost their appetite and taste for youthful pleasures, they soon forget that they once were young, and become incapable of granting that indulgence to those who are coming up into life, which they themselves in that situation would have thought perfectly reasonable. Or if they still retain an inclination towards those gaieties which the infirmities of age forbid them to enjoy, discontent and vexation, excited by the recollection of departed delights, incapacitate them for the generous satisfaction of participating, at secondhand, the pleasures of the young: envy becomes the parent of peevishness, and these passions are fed and nourished by those very circumstances which might afford them the most pleasing exercise of their benevolent affections. From these or other similar causes, aged persons often occasion endless vexations to themselves as well as to those who are under their controul, by censuring innocent mirth as childish folly; by fretting under the disturbance of diversions, in which with a better temper they might themselves find some amusement; and by refusing a trifling expence, or a small sacrifice of personal convenience, in procuring their young dependants a harmless gratification.

The

The errors both of the old and the young refpecting pleafure, may be corrected by viewing this object from the middle ftation of human life. Viewed from this ftation, the extreme fondnefs of the one, and the extreme difrelifh of the other, for pleafure will appear equally blameable. The delights of youth, being now contemplated in retrofpect, have loft the alluring charm of novelty, to which they owed fo much of their captivating power. Many circumftances, effentially neceffary to be taken into the account in judging of the value of pleafure, but commonly overlooked by thofe who are eager in the purfuit, are now diftinctly perceived: and it is found, upon the faireft examination of experience and reflection, that, although their object is entitled to fome fhare of attention as an occafional amufement and temporary gratification, it has no claim to be made the chief bufinefs of life; that, though the flowers with which pleafure ftrews our path may be be worth gathering, it is of little confequence whether the number be greater or smaller, in a path which is at best so short, and during a course, in which the discharge of our present duty, and our preparation for the subsequent periods of our existence, afford us so much serious business.

Another object concerning which the young and the aged, for the most part, differ very widely in their notions is, wealth. Generosity and liberality in the use of money may be reckoned among the characteristic virtues of young persons; economy and frugality among those of the old: and these easily degenerate, the former into prodigality, the latter into avarice. Unless particular pains be taken to inculcate upon young persons the lessons, and to form them to the habits of economy, it may be expected that they will rather value themselves upon the carelessness and profusion with which they squander away their property,

property, than upon their caution in expending, and their diligence in increasing their possessions. Having never reflected maturely on the various good purposes to which money is capable of being applied; having not yet experienced in themselves, nor taken much pains to observe in others, the fatal effects of extravagance; not being accustomed to look so far before them, as to be fully sensible of the importance of providing against the future exigencies of life; young people commonly despise those small attentions which economy requires, and value themselves upon a lavish waste of money, as a mark of a generous and noble spirit. In many instances, this destructive kind of vanity entices them not only to be lavish of their own property, or that of their parents, but to commit iniquitous depredations upon the property of the industrious tradesman, by contracting debts which they have no immediate and certain means of discharging. In the present artificial state of society there are exceptions to this general rule: there are young people who, even before the first affections of the heart have been allowed time to expand, have acquired such a fondness for the splendours of life, as to be willing to sacrifice its purest pleasures, and its most substantial blessings, in order to command those distinctions which wealth only can procure. But, except in the case of this premature depravation of sentiment and character, it will be commonly found the propensity of the young, rather to undervalue than to overvalue riches, and not only to look upon avarice as a sordid passion, but even to regard moderation and prudence as mean and ungenerous qualities.

The contrary extreme usually takes place in the character of old men. After having with great industry, and through a long course of years, been employed in in accumulating wealth, the object of their labours, of course, becomes the object of their affection. The precious ore which it has cost them so much pains to dig from the mine, shines in their eyes with heightened lustre. Comparing their own condition with that of others who have been less industrious and frugal, or less fortunate, they look down upon them with contempt, or with pity. Their own success gives them, as they imagine, a right to prescribe a prudent plan of life for the young, and to teach them from experience and observation the value of money. And it happens not unfrequently, that they enforce this lesson with a degree of rigour which deprives both themselves and their families of the liberal enjoyment of that wealth which they have taken so much pains to amass, and which excites, in the minds of the young, disgust and aversion against that prudent economy which it is intended to recommend.

What

What is the true medium between these extremes, may be easily perceived by viewing wealth from that period of life at which men have had sufficient experience of the value of riches, without having lost their relish for other enjoyments. At that period it will be clearly seen, that wealth, though, in the hands of a fool or a knave, an instrument of mischief to himself and others, under the direction of prudence and virtue, becomes a fruitful source of personal convenience and of public utility. At the same time it will be found an undoubted truth, confirmed by universal experience, that they are then alone worth possessing when they are obtained honestly, enjoyed with moderation, and applied to the purposes of beneficence.

If, in the next place, we consider the judgments which are formed by the young and the old concerning the *characters of men*, we shall find them widely different.

The

The opinion which we entertain of other men depends in some degree upon the judgment we form concerning ourselves. The young, who are seldom well skilled in the science of self-knowledge, or much practised in the exercise of self-examination, are commonly very well satisfied with themselves, and are thence disposed to be easily pleased with others. The amusing scenes of life furnish them with much more agreeable employment than that of moral speculation on the characters of men. Sincere and without disguise in their own professions and declarations, they cannot easily be brought to believe that all around them are not equally honest. Ever ready to lavish their kind affections upon others, they are loth to admit a suspicion that others are less open-hearted and generous than themselves. The good opinion they entertain of themselves lays them open to the artifices of adulation; and

they

they are readily perfuaded, that thofe who admire and flatter them muft be themfelves poffeffed of fuperior accomplifhments. They fancy themfelves every where furrounded with friends, and think every one who is poffeffed of an agreeable addrefs, and external embellifhments, worthy of a place in their efteem. If they look beyond the circle of their own connexions upon the general mafs of mankind, they are difpofed to allow to every man the degree of merit which he claims, and to believe that there is in the world much more virtue and happinefs than gloomy moralifts have been willing to admit. Notwithftanding fome untoward facts which are occafionally ftarting up to contradict the delightful theory, they affure themfelves that human nature is making a rapid progrefs towards perfection.

Place the fame picture before the old man, who views it with different eyes and

and under a different aspect, and a very different judgment will be formed. His long intercourse with the world has presented him with innumerable examples of fraud and wickedness; and he is so far from thinking men to be always what they seem, that he is persuaded they are scarcely ever such. This severe judgment is perhaps confirmed by a secret consciousness of obliquity in his own mind, and he seeks to find some palliation of his own dishonesty in the opinion that other men are at least as bad as himself. Or, without the supposition of criminality, we may conceive that the infirmities of age will serve to increase those jealousies and suspicions which knowledge of the world had raised; so that he now sees in every bargain a design to over-reach him, in every profession of regard some sinister purpose, and even under every expression of affection a selfish look towards his inheritance. With respect to the world at large, he
laments

laments that the decency, regularity, and moderation, which he remembers in his youthful days, are no longer to be found: he complains of the depravity of the age, and is much difpleafed to fee fo little refpect to authority, and fo little modefty and difcretion in the rifing generation. Fully perfuaded that the world, inftead of mending, is continually growing worfe, he perhaps pioufly confoles himfelf in the profpect of his approaching end with the thought that he fhall be mercifully taken away from the evil to come.

A middle judgment, equally diftant from the weak credulity of the young, and the cynical feverity of the aged, will be paffed by a wife man, who, viewing the world from the middle ftation of human life, will weigh in an even fcale the merits and the faults of mankind. If he finds himfelf compelled by innumerable facts to admit that there is more fraud and vice in the world than he formerly fuppofed; and if this extorted conviction teaches him

him the neceffity of uniting, in our intercourfe with the world, the wifdom of the ferpent with the innocence of the dove; all this, however, does not tempt him to think uncharitably of thofe of whofe fterling merit he has had reafonable proof, much lefs to treat with ingratitude thofe who have given him unequivocal teftimonies of perfonal efteem and friendfhip. If in any inftances he has met with hard returns for faithful fervice, or with unkind neglect and unmerited cenfure, far from inferring from fuch facts that all men are alike difingenuous, he will only on this account be the more attached to thofe whom his mature judgment approves as worthy of his firmeft confidence, and entitled to his moft cordial and grateful affection. In contemplating the general character of mankind, though his expectations, after a long experience of the defpotic fway which error, folly, and vice, have obtained, will be lefs fanguine than formerly, he will neverthelefs

find

find sufficient proofs of the general progress of knowledge to convince him that this single cause will at length, notwithstanding the powerful opposition of interest and bigotry, have sufficient energy to produce the universal improvement of mankind in every thing essential to the happiness of individuals, and of society.

It remains that we take a brief notice of the opposite opinions and sentiments of the young and the aged on the general condition of human life.

To young persons life commonly appears a shining and flowery spring, which yields a thousand present delights, and promises a summer richly laden with precious fruits. They have heard, indeed, that it sometimes happens that storms and tempests rise to darken the brightest sky; and they are told that the summer and autumn of mature life must be at length succeeded by the gloomy winter of age: but they think it wholly unnecessary to damp the ardour of their present pursuits

by

by turning their attention to events so uncertain or so remote. Their natural cheerfulness and gaiety of spirit has never been checked by any serious calamity. The presumption of their hopes has never been chastised by any sad experience of the fickleness of fortune. Their confidence in themselves has suffered no correction from the failure of hasty and ill-concerted projects. The flattering idea of self-importance, which in some degree hangs upon every human mind, operates with peculiar force upon the young, seducing them into a fond imagination that every one is attentive to their inclinations and interests, and that the world is busy in providing for their entertainment. From these and other causes, young people enter upon life with the most sanguine expectations of finding every relation an inexhaustible fund of delight, and of seeing all their schemes and enterprises crowned with success. They behold Fame standing ready to found

found the praise of their talents and merit, and Fortune waiting to reward their industry. Thus delighted with themselves and their prospects, they contemplate human life as an enchanting scene, inviting to action, pregnant with pleasure, and rich in hope; and they wonder at the peevishness and perverseness of those who can find in the world nothing but causes of vexation and complaint.

Such is human life viewed in prospect. Let us now for a moment consider how it appears in retrospect. The gay illusions of youthful fancy are now all vanished. The disappointed traveller has seen many a bright prospect overclouded with storms. In his way through life he has met with many disappointments and mortifications, perhaps with many heavy calamities. Plans which promised great things have failed. Those in whom he confided have deserted him. Some of the firmest pillars of his confidence on earth, on which he relied for support in his declining years, have

have been torn down. With all this appearance of the uncertainty and vanity of all earthly poffeffions, he is at length arrived at the period when youthful ftrength and beauty are exchanged for feeblenefs and deformity—when the fenfes are benumbed, and defire fails. With powers too languid for action, he takes little intereft in any thing that happens around him. Dead even to the finer feelings of affection, he only lives to lament that he no longer finds any thing on earth to love. The companions of his youth having dropped one after another into the grave, what wonder if at fourfcore he afks—" Where is the world into which I was born ?" What wonder if, with all his own experience of misfortune, and with his long obfervation of the ills of life, the world fhould appear to him a dreary wildernefs, and the air in which he breathes " a foul and peftilent congregation of vapours," if he fhould be ready, with fome feelings of fatiety and even difguft, gust, to say—" I loath it: I would not live always?"

If the former of these views of life be too gay, the latter is certainly too gloomy. The true medium is the aspect under which life is seen at the middle station in passing from youth to age. By the help of long experience and cool reflection, it is there clearly perceived that this world is neither a paradise of flowers, nor a wilderness of thorns; that though trouble and sorrow are the common lot of mortals, this sad account is, through the bounty of Divine Providence, commonly far overbalanced by enjoyments and gratifications of various kinds, animal, social, and intellectual. But that which above all tends to make us contented and thankful in our present condition, is the conviction which such an impartial survey of life will afford us, that our present state of existence is a course of moral discipline, conducted by our Almighty Parent, by a due improvement of which we may provide

vide ourselves with a fund of peaceful reflections and comfortable hopes, abundantly sufficient to cheer the vale of old age, and even to inspire us with serenity and peace in our last moments. The good man hath hope in his death.

As the proper practical application of the survey we have now taken of human life, let the young learn sobriety in their pursuit of pleasure, moderation in their expectation of happiness, and caution and prudence in forming and executing their plans of living; let those who are in the middle station of life be instructed to give all diligence to improve the precious days of active usefulness which yet remain to them; let the aged be cautioned against the infirmities of moroseness, censoriousness, and discontent, to which their period of life is more peculiarly liable, and exhorted to render their last days comfortable to themselves and to all about them, by easy affability, by cheerful good-humour; and, as long as the powers of action remain, by kind endeavours to serve and oblige: and, finally, let us all be taught so to number our days as to apply our hearts unto wisdom.

On Humility.

ROMANS xii. 3.

I say, through the grace given unto me, to every man that is among you, not to think of himself more highly than he ought to think.

To form an accurate judgment of things according to their real nature is a high and important attainment. With respect to natural bodies, it is this which chiefly distinguishes the philosopher from the vulgar observer of nature, and preserves him from mistakes and errors in the use and application of the objects around him to which the ignorant are continually liable. With respect to religion, it is this which distinguishes the rational worshipper of God from the enthusiast:

thusiast: the former conceiving justly of God and religion, the latter forming weak and erroneous notions, and indulging idle and visionary fancies, concerning both. But there is nothing in which a judgment perfectly conformable to nature and truth is more desirable than in the opinion we form concerning ourselves; for it is very evident, that if we entertain a wrong idea of our own natural powers, of our dispositions and character, or of our condition and connexions in life, we shall be in continual danger of being betrayed by our misapprehensions into injurious errors of conduct. This will be equally true, whether we think too highly or too meanly of ourselves. But because self-love commonly prevents the latter of these errors, the precepts of morality respecting this subject are most frequently directed against the former. The apostle Paul thought the caution against thinking too highly of ourselves of sufficient importance to warrant a particular solemnity of introduction

duction—" I say, through the grace given unto me, or in the exercise of my office and authority as an apostolic teacher of religion, to every man among you, not to think of himself more highly than he ought to think."

It is evidently required by this precept, in the first place, that we should not think ourselves possessed of virtues, accomplishments, or advantages, of which we are in reality destitute, or imagine our real attainments or possessions greater than they are. This is a point on which we are in great danger of falling into mistakes. Through the influence of that self-love, which easily degenerates into self-partiality, we take pleasure both in flattering ourselves, and in being flattered by others. We give easy credit to every appearance and every report which tends to raise us in our own esteem; but are exceedingly loth to observe, and even very industrious to conceal from our own observation, any circumstance which might

might tend to lower the good opinion we entertain of ourselves. This self-delusion might be in a great measure corrected, if we would honestly inform ourselves of the opinion which the world entertains of us; for this, when it can be truly obtained, will be seldom found to err on the side of candour. But, instead of listening with diligence to the intimations which either our friends or our enemies may be inclined to give us of our faults, and wisely applying them to the correction and improvement of our characters, we are too apt to receive every hint which implies a censure of our conduct with resentment; we immediately suspect that the person from whom it proceeds either judged weakly, is ill-informed, or has some evil intention; and hastily conclude, that whoever takes upon them to find fault with us, must either do it through ignorance or malice: and this conclusion we are too often encouraged to make by the injudicious partiality of friends, the unmeaning

meaning complaifance of general acquaintance, or the impofing flattery of interefted dependents. Some love us too well to fee our faults, or have too much regard for our friendfhip to hazard the lofs of it by mentioning them. Others treat us with great attention and refpect, not perhaps becaufe they are in truth perfuaded that we deferve it, but becaufe they are defirous of living upon good terms with us, or becaufe they are loth to violate the rules of civility and good-breeding: whilft a third clafs, from felfifh views, and with bafe hypocrify, make it their bufinefs to puff us up with a vain conceit of our fuperior accomplifhments: a deception to which perfons of every degree are more or lefs liable, and to which few perfons do not willingly yield. It requires little fkill to prepare, or caution to prefent, a cup which is fo generally palatable as that of flattery.

In this manner, and from thefe caufes, do we continually fee men fall into ftrange and

and astonishing errors in judging of their own characters: the ignorant, who have never given themselves the trouble to examine the ground of any one opinion which they hold, fancying themselves possessed of superior knowledge and wisdom, and issuing forth their bold assertions with an authoritative and dogmatical air: the devoted slaves of avarice, whose bosoms are strangers to every sentiment of generosity and humanity, persuading themselves that they are good christians; and men whose daily intemperance, dishonesty, or cruelty, refute every pretension to religion, valuing themselves for their piety and zeal. And where men do not so entirely mistake their own characters as to applaud themselves for excellencies to which they are wholly strangers, nothing is more common than to magnify in their conceptions their own accomplishments and virtues, and imagine themselves entitled to the highest esteem for qualities, in which they are in fact excelled by many

many others, or in which, after all, they are very deficient. We eafily remark this in others, but ftrangely overlook it in ourfelves; and yet, perhaps, there is fcarcely an individual among us, who, if he will probe his heart to the bottom, may not find within himfelf the feeds of vanity, and convince himfelf that, in many particulars, he thinks of himfelf more highly than he ought to think. It is poffible, indeed, for a man to think too meanly of himfelf; and wherever, through natural timidity of temper, exceffive modefty, or erroneous opinions in religion or morals, this happens, the miftake ought to be corrected, both for a man's own comfort, and for the benefit of fociety. But the common danger unqueftionably is, that we fhould think too well of ourfelves; and, therefore, we fhould exercife the utmoft care that we neither indulge conceit and vanity ourfelves, nor fuffer it to be cherifhed by others. We fhould be as ready to liften to the faithful admonitions

tions of friendship as to the soothing insinuations of flattery: we should even be willing to learn our faults from those who are most inclined from ill-will to expose them, remembering that it is wise to suffer ourselves to be instructed even by an enemy. But our first concern should be to be faithful to ourselves, and to weigh our own characters in the balance of impartial judgment.

Further, if we be desirous to comply with the precept of the text, we must be careful not to think more highly of our real accomplishments or possessions than they deserve. Whatever be our endowments, we should value them only in proportion to their intrinsic worth.

If we be in truth possessed of genuine piety and goodness, we have a right to regard these qualities as inestimable treasures; for they are the only sure foundation of happiness, and the best title to applause. Virtue, wherever it is seen, must be loved and revered: all good beings
admire

admire it, and God himſelf looks down upon it with complacency. It is, then, no violation of moral propriety, or of the chriſtian law of humility, for the good man to be ſatisfied from himſelf. It is poſſible, however, to value ourſelves too highly even for our virtues. A virtuous temper and conduct is no more than may reaſonably be expected from every man; no more than is required from every man, as the proof of his allegiance to the Sovereign of the univerſe. " When ye ſhall have done all thoſe things which are commanded you, ſay, We are unprofitable ſervants, we have done that which it was our duty to do." Conſidering the manifeſt reaſonableneſs of virtue, it may rather be thought ſurpriſing that men ſhould act ill, than it ſhould be made a matter of admiration when they act well. When any man is inclined to boaſt of his merit, and to contemplate his own virtues with aſtoniſhment, it affords a preſumption that he has taken upon him a

new

new character, which he finds it difficult to support, and of which he is but imperfectly master. Those who have been long established in the habits of goodness, are too well acquainted with the extent of moral duty, and too sensible of their remaining defects, to be proud even of their virtues.

As we ought not to value ourselves too highly for our moral qualities, so neither for our intellectual attainments. Knowledge is unquestionably a valuable accomplishment, and a just ground of distinction, but it deserves praise chiefly on account of its usefulness; and the man who rests in the cultivation of his understanding as an ultimate object, and is more concerned to display it for the sake of the honour it may obtain him than to apply it to the benefit of others, has greater reason to be humble on account of his moral defects than to be proud of his mental acquisitions. When knowledge is of that kind which "puffeth up," we may be
assured

assured that it is either imaginary or superficial; for the more any man really knows, the more will he be sensible both of the imperfection of his present attainments, and of the vast extent of those fields of knowledge of which he has hitherto obtained only a faint and distant prospect.

Still less ought we to be vain of any of the exterior ornaments or distinctions of life. It is a common thing, indeed, for men to think highly of themselves on account of their high birth or great riches. But what is a noble descent, or ancient family, without personal merit? What right has he to be proud who, instead of being able to rank himself among the wise and good, can only rank himself among those great men who have disgraced their descent by their vices? "How much more honourable is it to be useful in the lowest condition, than to be insignificant and mischievous in the highest?" With respect to wealth, of what value is it it except for its use? or on what pretence can that man be vain of his possessions, who, instead of having acquired them by laudable methods, and applied them to beneficial purposes, only possesses the wages of iniquity, and uses them as instruments of vice? Be it ever so little that a righteous man hath, it is a better treasure, and affords a juster ground of boasting, than all the revenues that were ever amassed by extortion and oppression.

In order to preserve us from thinking of ourselves more highly than we ought to think, it will be necessary that, at the same time that we form a true estimate of our accomplishments and advantages, we have a just sense of our deficiencies and imperfections. To balance these fairly one against the other is as necessary in judging of ourselves, as it is for a merchant in estimating his real property to place his debts against his demands and present possessions. It often happens, that foibles and faults are so interwoven with accomplishments and excellencies in the same characters, that it is difficult to say whether they are more to be admired for the latter than blamed for the former; and since absolute perfection is unattainable by mortals, some spots are found even on the brightest character to diminish its lustre; the whitest robe of virtue, which any human being can boast, is stained with some blemishes. Not to take notice of these, is evidently to form a partial and deceitful judgment—" to think of ourselves more highly than we ought to think."

There is, moreover, some hazard of falling into this error when we compare ourselves with other men. If we wish neither to impose upon ourselves, nor to do injustice to others, it is very obvious, that when we attempt to compare their characters with our own, we should be very careful, in the first place, to have an accurate knowledge of both, and then to weigh in an even balance, and with a steady hand, excellencies against excellencies, and defects against defects. But in each of these undertakings there is more difficulty than may be at first apprehended. Our opportunities of becoming acquainted with the real dispositions and characters of men are so few, and we are so apt to view them through some deceitful medium either of affection or aversion, that we can seldom be sure that we form an exact opinion and fair judgment of any character. But supposing this to be accomplished, when we proceed to the comparison new dangers arise. Self-partiality will incline us to think the qualities in which we excel of greater intrinsic value than those by which others are distinguished; to prefer brilliant accomplishments in ourselves to solid virtues and useful attainments in others; to disguise our own faults under the gentle appellation of foibles and infirmities, and condemn those of our neighbour as grievous offences; in fine,

fine, so to adjust the articles of merit and demerit which are to be weighed against each other, or so to manage the beam of judgment by which they are to be weighed, as to make our own scale preponderate. The uncertainty and difficulty attending comparisons of this kind should make us sparing and cautious in the use of them. We should be very careful not to finish the comparison just at that point where we shall be most strongly tempted to finish it, when we have gone through such particulars of the examination as we had a previous expectation would turn out in our favour; but to go on, fairly and honestly, to such articles of comparison as, however humiliating, may afford us useful lessons of admonition and instruction. We should be careful, too, that we do not content ourselves with looking merely at our inferiors in character or condition; for in this way there are few persons who might not find means to swell their bosoms with pride and conceit;

ceit; but that we often look up to those whom we ourselves, with all our vanity, must confess to be our superiors in merit and accomplishments; and this we should do, by no means to awaken the troublesome feelings of envy, but to excite our emulation, and to teach us humility.

These precautions, diligently observed, will effectually repress the ebullitions of pride and vanity; and while they leave us possessed of a modest sense of our own merit, will give us a humble conviction of our numerous defects, and preserve us from "thinking of ourselves more highly than we ought to think."

Humility, thus become the settled temper and habit of our minds, this amiable disposition will influence us in our behaviour towards all men, whether they be our superiors, our equals, or our inferiors.

With respect to our superiors, let us be taught by the lesson of the text cheerfully to pay them all that respect and deference which,

which, either on account of exalted station, delegated power, or distinguished merit, is their due. To those who, on account of their superior talents, or for any other good reason, are entrusted with the administration of important offices for the public good, let us willingly pay that submission and obedience which their office entitles them to expect. To those who are our superiors in natural understanding, or acquired knowledge, let us yield the tribute of respectful attention to their opinions and arguments, and of reasonable, though not implicit, deference to their judgment. Those who are eminent for firm and invincible integrity, and active disinterested benevolence, let us contemplate with affectionate esteem, and not think it beneath us to make them the objects of our diligent imitation. In fine, whatever just ground of pre-eminence any one may have over us, let us cheerfully acquiesce in it, without artfully endeavouring to depreciate others in order to exalt ourselves to their level.

With respect to our equals, let humility teach us to live with them upon the easy and pleasant terms of mutual civility and condescension. If we have learned " not to think of ourselves more highly than we ought to think," we shall find no difficulty in obeying a subsequent precept, " Be kindly affectioned one towards another with brotherly love, in honour preferring one another." Instead of demanding from others that attention and respect which we are unwilling to bestow, we shall be ever ready to set the example of courteous and obliging behaviour. Instead of insisting upon a preference in cases where others have equal pretensions, and being offended when every thing does not give way to our humours or interests, we shall cheerfully yield to the claims of others, as far as it can be done with tolerable convenience and propriety. We shall neither be chagrined when more attention is paid by our superiors to others than to ourselves, nor offended if our acquaintance and friends, in any cafe, omit without defign the accuftomed expreffions of civility or refpect. Confcious of our own defects, we fhall never expect perfection in others.

In the laft place, having learned the leffon of the text, let it render us affable and courteous towards our inferiors. If any of us be placed in civil relations which imply dominion, and require the exercife of power, let us confider the offices of fociety as appointed, not for the fake of exalting the perfons who govern, but for benefiting thofe who are governed, and let us be careful to avoid every appearance of that " infolence of office" which is more burdenfome than the authority of law. If we are called to exercife that power which nature has connected with the parental relation, let us temper the aufterity of command, and the rigour of difcipline, with the gentlenefs and tendernefs of affection. With refpect to thofe over whom we have no other fuperiority than

than that which arifes from the accidental diftinctions of fortune, let humility incline us rather to diminifh the diftance by eafy familiarity, than to increafe it by diftant referve or affected condefcenfion. No one wifhes to be put in mind of his inferiority; and this may be almoft as effectually done by taking great pains to convince thofe whom we notice that we are condefcending to treat them with civility, as by the moft open claims of fuperiority, or the moft haughty airs of confequence. Thofe people whofe pride renders them incapable of fpeaking to an inferior but with a tone and manner which intimates their importance, are infolent even in their condefcenfions. True affability confifts in concealing fuperiority under the pleafing veil of eafy freedom: genuine humility, in never expecting any other tribute of refpect than fuch as men are inclined to pay from inward efteem and affection. Nothing can juftify the arrogance with which fome men

men extort homage from their inferiors, or excufe the infolent contempt with which they fometimes treat them. If things be meafured by the rule of reafon, what is the boafted diftance between the higheft and the loweft of mankind ? Are not the higheft and the loweft partakers of one common nature, with all its diftinguifhing excellencies, and all its peculiar frailties and imperfections? If the rich man is by nature rational, intelligent, and capable of wifdom, virtue, and happinefs, the poor man poffeffes the fame faculties. If the rich man is by nature free, and poffeffed of unalienable rights, the poor man is endowed with the fame facred poffeffion. If the rich man is the offspring of God, enjoys the protection of his providence in this world, and looks forward to an everlafting inheritance in the world to come ; the poor man, too, has God for his father and protector, and, if he obey and ferve him on earth, is heir of an eternal inheritance. On the other hand, is the poor man continually dependent

pendent upon his fellow-creatures, upon nature, and upon the God of nature, for his support? Is he liable to error and prejudice, to folly and vice? Is he exposed to accident, to disease, to disappointment, and sorrow? And must all the cares, and labours, and enjoyments, of his short and precarious existence on earth, terminate in the grave? Such, too, is the condition of the rich. In one common lot of good and evil the rich and the poor meet together; for the Lord is the maker of us all. What right, then, can the rich have to treat the poor with insolence or contempt? Let them ever remember, that the world was not made for them alone, but for the common support and benefit of the whole; that God hath made of one blood all nations of men to dwell on all the face of the earth; and that the day is approaching when all men must appear on an equal footing in the presence of him who accepteth not the persons of men, nor regardeth the rich more than the poor.

The Value of Moral Wisdom.

PROVERBS iv. 17.

Wisdom is the principal thing; therefore get wisdom.

IF Solomon had said, "Wealth is the principal thing, therefore get wealth," his doctrine would have been better relished, and obtained more credit. And yet Solomon has long been ranked amongst the wisest of men, and therefore, probably, had some good reason for the judgment which he here gives in favour of wisdom. Thus much respect, at least, is due to his opinion, that we

should

should attentively examine the grounds upon which this judgment is built, and confider how far it merits our practical regard in the conduct of life.

The inquiry every one muft allow to be exceedingly interefting. For if, through precipitation in forming our own opinion, or through an implicit reliance upon that of others, we feek our happinefs from fources whence it cannot be derived, difappointment and infelicity muft inevitably be the iffue. And no one, who obferves the marks of difcontent which appear through every rank and ftation of life, can think that men are already fo univerfally and perfectly fkilled in the art of happinefs, as to render the inquiry unneceffary. To thofe who are already confiderably advanced in the path of life, it cannot be amifs to ftand ftill and afk themfelves, whether they are in the right way. To thofe who are juft entering upon the world, and have a character to form and a condition,

dition, both in this world and another, to fix for themfelves, it muft be of infinite moment, to make a true judgment concerning the main ends of living, and the chief bufinefs of man. Let us, then, examine with diligent attention the confiderations which, probably, led Solomon to lay it down as a decided maxim, that " wifdom is the principal thing."

Wifdom, in its general idea, is the clear difcernment, and the determined choice of the beft ends, and of the fitteft means to accomplifh them. As it refpects the conduct of life, wifdom confifts in an accurate knowledge of the nature of human happinefs, and in the firm adoption, and fteady purfuit, of thofe meafures by which it is to be attained.

Can it be queftioned, whether this moral wifdom be an object above all others, moft worthy of our purfuit? If there be any value in human life; if there be any difference between being happy and

and being wretched, it muſt be our *firſt* concern, to make choice of a kind of happineſs which is ſuited to our nature, and which lies within the reach of our faculties, and our *next*, to acquaint ourſelves with the means by which this happineſs may be acquired. He who endeavours to be happy in any way, which the conſtitution of man, and the laws of nature forbid, is perpetually contending with impoſſibilities, and therefore muſt " labour in vain, and ſpend his ſtrength for nought." If, then, we wiſh to eſcape the moſt fatal diſappointment, that which would ariſe from the failure of our plan of happineſs, we muſt exerciſe judgment in the choice of proper objects of purſuit, and diſcretion in the ſelection and uſe of adequate means to attain them; that is, we muſt cultivate moral wiſdom.

That we may have ſtill farther proofs of the value of moral wiſdom, let us diſtinctly

tinctly confider feveral of thofe gifts of nature or fortune, which are commonly looked upon as fources or means of happinefs, and obferve how neceffary it is, in order to render them real bleffings, that they fhould be under the direction of wifdom.

An affluent fortune, agreeable connections, a healthful conftitution, and a found underftanding, may afford a man the means and the capacity of enjoyment; but, unlefs he has the difcretion to manage and improve them, they will not of themfelves make him happy.

Even in the *acquifition* of riches, if we look beyond mere poffeffion, to enjoyment, fomething farther is neceffary, than that kind of policy which is called worldly wifdom. For it is impoffible that any man, who has not banifhed from his bofom every notion of integrity, and every fentiment of humanity, fhould be capable of enjoying poffeffions which he has obtained by injuftice, oppreffion, and cruelty. But, in order to enjoy riches, it is not only neceffary, that we be confcious of having acquired them by honeft means, but that we be poffeffed of thofe difpofitions and habits which will enable us to relifh, as well as to incite us to purfue, the feveral fpecies of gratification they are capable of affording. If we confider only the loweft and moft vulgar ufe of riches, that of plentifully furnifhing us with luxuries for the indulgence of our animal appetites, it muft require fome difcretion, to confine ourfelves within fuch bounds, in partaking of the ftores which nature and fortune have provided for us, as fhall not be deftructive of our health, and, confequently, of our capacity for enjoyment. For want of that prudence which is the parent of temperance, many a favourite of fortune, whofe fplendid manner of living attracts the admiration and envy of thoufands.

sands beneath him, is daily tantalized with the sight of luxuries, which a diseased constitution will not permit him to enjoy.

But if we regard wealth as instrumental in opening to us new sources of intellectual entertainment, and moral satisfaction, it becomes still more necessary, that we call in the aid of wisdom, to enable us to make an advantageous use of our possessions.

Wealth may give a man the free command of his time, but it is wisdom alone which can teach him how to employ it. Leisure is no benefit to those, who, for want of a mind well-informed and principled by education, have no desire to increase their knowledge, or improve their sentiments, by reading and reflection. Such persons must be wholly dependent upon external objects for their enjoyments. Time will hang upon them as a heavy burden, which must, at all events, be shaken off. Hence, under the notion of passing away time, they will have recourse to amusements, which frequent repetition will render insipid; or to low and intemperate pleasures, which must, in the issue, prove disgraceful and ruinous. They only, who have learned to exercise their rational faculties, and to regulate their thoughts and affections, are qualified to make a proper distribution of those portions of time which are left at their own disposal. It is the wise man alone, who, when he has no necessary business upon his hands, will know what to do.

Riches are, moreover, capable of yielding the pure and exalted pleasure of doing good; but they can only produce this precious fruit in an enlightened and cultivated mind. Ignorance and selfishness are nearly allied. It is not to be expected, that the man who has never raised his conceptions above the objects of sense, and employed his faculties in contemplat-

ing

ing the nature of man, the connexions of fociety, and the moral obligations arifing from thefe, fhould have any fixed principle of benevolence, or any fteady and habitual defire of being ufeful to his fellow-creatures. Nature has, indeed, fown the feeds of humanity, more or lefs liberally, in every breaft; but they cannot fpring up and flourifh without the aid of cultivation. Unlefs the plant, upon its firft appearance, be carefully protected and induftrioufly cultivated, it will foon be overrun by the weeds of felfifh paffions, or trampled under foot by indolence. Accordingly, we fee in fact, that where education has done nothing more for young men, than put them into the beaten track again; where parents, who have themfelves had no other ideas than thofe of getting and faving, have had no ambition that their children fhould look farther, they commonly purfue the narrow road of felf-intereft interest without the smallest deviation, till their accumulated treasures invite them to enlarge their plan of living, and adopt new modes of expence; and that, when this welcome period arrives, they adopt a system of economy, which, whilst it provides for every kind of private indulgence which appetite, whim, or vanity, could suggest, makes no provision for gratifying the best feelings of the heart, those of benevolence. Through a pitiful ambition of displaying their wealth, they load their tables with a profusion of luxuries greater than can possibly be enjoyed; they encumber themselves with an idle retinue, who, whilst they ape every folly of their masters, are perpetually preying upon their property; they adorn their mansions with expensive productions of art, which they have not taste enough to relish; they spare no cost in enlarging and improving their domains, that they may enjoy, at second-

second-hand, the delight and admiration which they themselves do not feel; they engage in a perpetual round of private and public amusements, which, for want of an improved understanding and cultivated taste, afford them no other pleasure than that which arises from being seen among a fashionable crowd. In the mean time, they allot no part of that vast fund which is capable of supporting so many superfluous expences, to the purposes of private charity, or public utility. And why? Because they are strangers to that " wisdom which is from above," which " is—full of mercy and of good fruits." The truth is, that a solid foundation for generosity and public spirit can only be laid in just principles of morals, enlarged views of human life, and an habitual sense of religious obligation. The wise man alone will be uniformly and consistently good, and is, therefore, alone capable of enjoying in perfection the pleasures of beneficence.

If from external possessions we turn our attention, in the next place, to our social connexions, we shall find that these will afford us no true happiness, unless we are possessed of wisdom.

The powerful ties of natural affection, which form the chief bond of union in the domestic relations, are evidently intended by our Creator to be among the chief sources of human happiness. But, in order to render them effectually such, they must be cultivated by wisdom and directed by prudence. Where this culture and regulation is neglected, it is universally seen, either that these relations are not formed, or that they are not productive of felicity. If the foundation of a domestic character be not early laid—if the domestic virtues be not early implanted in the heart, by precept, discipline, and example; there is great reason to apprehend that young persons will be seduced into a course of life, which will wholly banish from their bosoms every tender sentiment and *virtuous* affection, and thus at once disqualify and indispose them for entering upon the relations of domestic life: or, if they should be so fortunate as to escape seduction, it is by no means improbable, that, for want of being *early* moulded by the hand of wisdom, they will acquire opinions and maxims, or fall into habits, which will destroy the peace and comfort of their domestic connexions. Every one, who forms a connexion of this kind, expects it to be a happy one. Whence comes it to pass, that this expectation is so frequently frustrated?—Undoubtedly, from the want of moral and religious wisdom. Young persons are early habituated to set an excessive value upon exterior accomplishments; and are seldom sufficiently instructed, either by the lessons of those who have had more experience than themselves, or by their own reflections,

reflections, in the superior importance of intellectual and moral merit. Hence it frequently happens, that, in the most interesting subject of deliberation which can ever come before them, they pay little attention to those circumstances which ought chiefly to direct their choice; the consequence of which must often be, the most mortifying and distressing disappointment. To the same source we may trace back those dissensions and animosities, which so frequently disturb the peace, and destroy the happiness of families. These universally arise from misapprehension and wrong judgment in one, at least, of the parties; or from the indulgence of unreasonable desires, perverse humours, or disorderly passions, which an accurate acquaintance with the nature, and a just sense of the importance, of moral obligation might have corrected. The unsuccessfulness of education, so often lamented by disappointed and

and unhappy parents, is commonly to be ascribed to the same cause. Were parents themselves well instructed in the principles of religious and moral wisdom, and duly sensible of the necessity of well-regulated affections and virtuous habits, to the happiness of human life, it would be impossible that they should be inattentive to the great concern of forming the dispositions and manners of their children. They would then be in little danger of mistaking unseasonable and improper indulgence for real kindness, or of substituting an unnecessary and vexatious severity in the room of a cool and steady discipline. Their anxious cares and labours would not then be wholly employed in providing them with the means of making a splendid appearance, or furnishing them with external decorations and accomplishments. Convinced that the happiness of their children, as well as their own, must depend chiefly upon the

the habit and temper of the mind, and upon a capacity of relishing intellectual, moral, and religious pleasures, they would be chiefly concerned to give them habits of industry, self-command, contentment, and good-humour, to inspire them with sentiments of honour, integrity, generosity, and piety, and to furnish them with plentiful stores of useful knowledge. The natural consequence would be—a consequence which could scarcely be prevented by any subsequent change of situation—that their children would rise up into life, to experience the pleasures, and to reap the honours and rewards, of wisdom and virtue. " Train up a child in the way in which he should go, and when he is old, he will not depart from it."

It were easy to apply the doctrine of the text to every other connexion of social life. Who does not see, for example, that the pleasures of friendship can only be be enjoyed in perfection by those whom wisdom has taught to distinguish the reality from the semblance of esteem and affection, inspired with all those generous sentiments and kind propensities which alone can kindle and cherish the sacred flame? Who does not perceive, that the comforts and satisfactions of mutual intercourse among neighbours and acquaintance must depend upon the mutual exercise of civility, candour, moderation, generosity, and all those kind affections and good offices, which are the natural offspring of a mind well instructed in the precepts and deeply tinctured with the principles of wisdom? In fine, who can need to be informed, that most of the disorders which arise in civil communities are the effect of passions which it is the office of wisdom to subdue; and that if all men had right conceptions of the nature of the several relations which subsist in society, and a just apprehension of the obligations which result from these, universal verfal peace and harmony would naturally enfue?

If, in the laſt place, we examine thoſe ſources of happineſs which every man enjoys *within* himſelf, we ſhall immediately perceive that theſe, as well as all external good things, are able to make us happy only ſo far as they are under the direction of wiſdom.

Health of body, which is ſo juſtly conſidered as an invaluable bleſſing, can only be preſerved by following thoſe laws of regularity and temperance which wiſdom preſcribes; and, whilſt it is enjoyed, it is only the exerciſe of prudence and ſelf-command which can give us the full poſſeſſion of its comforts. If the vigour and cheerfulneſs which health naturally inſpires be not regulated by diſcretion, and chaſtened by ſobriety, they may betray us into diſgraceful follies or deſtructive vices.

With reſpect to thoſe enjoyments which are immediately derived from and feated in the mind, it is evident that they are, in their very nature, true wifdom. When we exercife our intellectual faculties on objects fuited to our abilities and opportunities, and with a degree of diligence and affiduity proportioned to their importance, that is, when we employ our underftandings judicioufly and wifely, we derive from the immediate exercife true and refined enjoyment. When we exert our active powers, and give fcope to our affections and paffions in that direction and degree which the nature of the objects around us and our own fituation require, that is, in the direction and degree which wifdom dictates, we experience immediate pleafure, as well as reap certain benefit. All the inconveniences which men fuffer from their appetites and paffions are the fruits of fome mifapprehenfion either concerning the nature of happinefs, or concerning the means of attaining it, that is, are the effects of folly. " When wifdom entereth into thine heart,"

heart," faith Solomon, "and knowledge is pleafant to thy foul, difcretion fhall preferve thee, underftanding fhall keep thee."

It appears, then, as the refult of all that hath been advanced in this difcourfe, that there is nothing upon which human happinefs fo much depends as upon an accurate knowledge, and a deep fenfe of our duty, or, in the words of the text, that "wifdom is the principal thing."

The inference fuggefted by Solomon is the moft natural which can poffibly be deduced from the doctrine we have been eftablifhing—" Therefore get wifdom, and with all thy getting get underftanding."

It hath pleafed Almighty God, my brethren, to afford you many opportunities and advantages for making this important acquifition. Be it your conftant concern to improve them, with a degree of diligence proportioned to the value of the object. Let thofe of you who have been

been early conducted into the path of wifdom by the hand of virtuous and religious Education, be thankful to Divine Providence for fo diftinguifhed a privilege. Let the young, who ftill enjoy the benefit of wife inftruction, feafonable admonition, and good examples from their parents and preceptors, fet a juft value on the advantages they poffefs; and, inftead of complaining and murmuring under the yoke of authority, let them rejoice that they have it in their power to correct the errors of their own judgment, and to fupply the defects of their own experience, by the knowledge and wifdom of thofe whom time and obfervation muft have qualified, and whom intereft and affection muft incline, to conduct them in the right path. "Hear, ye children, the inftructions of your parents, and attend to know underftanding." And let thofe who have paffed the years of juvenile inftruction, or have been in any meafure deftitute of the benefits of education, induftrioufly improve the opportunities which they at prefent enjoy for acquiring a more perfect knowledge of their duty. Let your eyes be ever open to what paffes in the world, not to furnifh you with matter for uncharitable reflections, but to enable you to collect ufeful inftructions from the virtues, and feafonable warnings from the follies and vices, of others. Let your ears be ever attentive to the cafual fuggeftions of good fenfe and prudence in converfation, and efpecially to the faithful admonitions of friendfhip. Employ fome ftated portions of the leifure which you are able to command, be it more or lefs, (for fome leifure it is in the power of every one to command) in making yourfelves acquainted with fuch writings as treat of religious and moral fubjects in the cleareft and moft interefting manner: efpecially ftudy that facred volume which abounds with every fpecies of moral and religious inftruction. "Search the fcriptures, which are able to make you wife unto falvation."

salvation." In fine, attend diligently to the lessons of instruction, exhortation, and admonition, which are delivered to you at stated seasons; always endeavouring to carry away with you, from time to time, some useful information, or some good impression, that " ye may not be forgetful hearers but doers of the word."

In this manner, my brethren, in the midst of all your ardour in the search after pleasure, and all your cares and labours to acquire riches, " get wisdom, and with all your getting get understanding.—Watch daily at the gates of wisdom, and wait at the posts of her doors: for whoso findeth wisdom findeth life, and shall obtain favour of the Lord."

Which, &c.

On the Necessity of establishing good Principles, and fixing a prudent Plan of Conduct, in early Life.

PROVERBS iv. 26.

Ponder the path of thy feet, that all thy ways may be established.

THERE is not in human life a more interesting period than that which lies between childhood and mature age. In this period chiefly it is that the character of the future man is formed, and that the seeds of his future honour or disgrace, happiness or misery, are sown. At its commencement childish sports and amusements

ments lose their charm, and are left behind as no longer deserving of attention; and the young adventurer presses forward, not without some degree of impatience, into the spacious field of new pursuits which lies before him. He promises himself enjoyment, distinction, felicity.

To damp his ardour by foreboding disappointment and vexation would be as injudicious as it would be unkind: for though many young persons, who have set out in life with high expectations, have been in a short time lost to themselves and the world, this has almost always happened through some folly or misconduct of their own or their friends. Where the soil is good, and the culture skilful and industrious, a plentiful harvest may be commonly expected.

It is, however, at this season, absolutely necessary that young persons should find leisure for serious reflections on their nature, expectations, and duties. Entering upon a world in which they must rely upon their own judgment, prudence, and resolution, much more than upon the kindness of others, for their happiness, and in which every valuable interest must depend upon their judging rightly and acting well; it must be their wisdom for a while to interrupt their favourite pursuits, and call off their attention from the agreeable objects around them, in order to fix upon a plan of conduct which they may safely follow through life, and which will leave them no room for self-reproach at the close of their days.

Whatever the conduct of the thoughtless, who live "at all adventures," may seem to imply, nothing can be more certain than that man was not born to trifle. Many seem to treat human life as an idle jest—a farce so insignificant, that it is of no moment whether it be acted well or ill: but the constitution of our nature is such, that it will not permit us to be mere cyphers in the creation. Serious happiness, or serious misery, must be the portion

portion of every man for himfelf, and muft be conveyed through his hands to others.

Man is endued with bodily fenfes and mental powers, which muft unavoidably be the fource either of enjoyment or fuffering, in various forms, through the whole of his exiftence; and whether they fhall be the one or the other, is a point which no one, who thinks at all, can regard with indifference.

It cannot appear a matter of no confequence whether his body fhall continue to old age in an healthful ftate, capable of active exertions and a lively relifh of enjoyment, or fhall be tortured with pain, or emaciated by difeafe. It is not in the power of any man to view all the ftores which nature and art have provided for our fupport, convenience, and gratification, with fuch perfect unconcern as to be wholly indifferent whether he pafs his days in the midft of abundance, or pine away a tirefome exiftence in want and wretchedness. Contemplating himself merely as an animal being, life must appear of some value to every man.

But if we turn our attention to our rational nature, and reflect upon the extent and variety of our intellectual and active faculties, we shall perceive our existence rising in value, and feel that we have important interests depending upon every inquiry concerning the happiness of man.

To a being capable of distinguishing truth from error, and of deriving pleasure from the pursuit and attainment of knowledge, it must be of some moment to be in a situation in which he can prosecute his researches with advantage; preserve and cherish an ardent thirst after knowledge, and be free from the influence of prejudices which would pervert his judgment, and of passions which would obstruct his inquiries. To a being endued with a love of reputation, and with many social affections, which necessarily render him

him dependent upon his fellow-creatures for a large portion of his happinefs, it muſt be an object deſerving his moſt ſerious attention to preſerve his mind in a ſtate well diſpoſed to derive enjoyment from the friendly intercourſes of ſociety, and from acts of beneficence and humanity; and to guard againſt all thoſe perverſe humours and malignant paſſions which would at once incapacitate him for ſocial enjoyment, and render him an object of averſion or contempt to the world. Laſtly, to a being whoſe faculties enable him to diſcern in every thing around him the traces of intelligence and deſign, and to diſcover the God of Nature in his works, and who, in conſequence hereof, can exerciſe the affections of religious veneration and gratitude, and experience the pleaſures of devotion, it cannot be a matter of indifference whether he ſhall remain in ſuch a ſtate of ignorance as to be wholly incapable of pious contemplations and exerciſes; whether his conceptions

tions of the Deity fhall be fo clouded by fuperftition as to render his religious feelings rather a fource of terror than enjoyment; or whether he fhall have fuch conceptions of the divine nature, and fuch habits of piety, as fhall give ftrength and elevation to his virtue, and afford him an inexhauftible fund of peace and confolation.

If human nature be confidered in thefe different points of view, as capable of animal, intellectual, focial, moral, and religious pleafures, the exiftence of man, even during the fhort period allotted to him in the prefent world, muft appear a valuable treafure, which it would be madnefs not to employ to the beft advantage in his power.

If life be thus important with refpect to every human being taken individually, how much does it rife in confequence when we furvey the numerous relations and dependencies which nature has eftablifhed among mankind!

It

It is not in the power of any man to live to himself alone. We come into the world surrounded with interesting connexions, and our conduct must materially affect the condition and character of all to whom we are related. Parents, kindred, teachers, and friends, are deeply interested in the happiness of the rising race, and cannot be indifferent spectators of their actions. Their first expressions of amiable qualities, in those days of infant simplicity when reflection has not matured them into virtues, afford the virtuous parent pleasures not to be expressed; and their little follies, before knowledge and experience have given them the power of being vicious, often touch their hearts with feelings of distress. At a more advanced period parental affection watches the growth of every fruitful plant, and of every noxious weed, with an anxious eye. A young man cannot discover the marks of an honest, prudent, and ingenuous mind, without giving his parents

the

the most lively impressions of satisfaction: he cannot fall into the vices of the licentious and profane, without "piercing them through with many sorrows." At his entrance upon active life, the circle of his connexions will be enlarging, and with it the influence of his conduct. When he forms new domestic relations of his own, he will hereby unavoidably extend his power of conferring happiness, or inflicting misery, upon others. The prosperity of a family, the personal happiness of the individuals who shall compose it, the character and condition of multitudes yet unborn, will probably, in this case, in a great measure depend upon him. The habits he now acquires, the temper he now forms, the course of life he now leads, will unavoidably operate to the advantage or the disadvantage, the pleasure or the pain, of all with whom he shall be connected in future life.

It is also a consideration which ought to have great weight with every young person,

person, that his future character must necessarily affect the happiness of the community to which he belongs. Every man, how narrow soever his sphere of life may be, contributes his part towards forming the public character; directly, by the virtues or vices which he practises; and indirectly, by the influence of his example upon his dependents and associates. Every good man is in this view a friend, and every bad man an enemy, to his country. But, besides this, the bond of union which subsists between the several members of a community, whilst it affords each individual important advantages, lays him under powerful obligations to exert his best talents for the public good.

Young persons, therefore, at their entrance upon the world, instead of consulting, as they are too apt to do, merely their own inclinations and humours, should inquire in what manner they may best contribute to the good order and prosperity

prosperity of the neighbourhood, and the community with which they are connected. Extending their views beyond the small circle of their personal interests, expanding their hearts with generous sentiments towards all around them, they should form their social connexions under a strong conviction of their obligation to live for others as well as themselves; with a warm desire of rendering themselves agreeable and useful in the circle of their acquaintance; with a fixed determination to employ their talents, as opportunity offers, in the service of their country and their species; and, in a word, under the powerful influence of a genuine spirit of patriotism and philanthropy.

To a young man, who thus considers himself, not as an insulated individual, but as related to a community in which the great end of public prosperity is to be pursued by the united efforts of its several members, and as belonging to a race of beings who are capable of continual advancement

vancement in knowledge, virtue, and happiness, it is impossible that his situation as a member of society, and as a human being, should not appear interesting and respectable—that life should not appear an object of high importance.

But the present state of man appears most of all important when it is regarded, not as the whole of his existence, but as introductory to a future eternal life. The doctrine of immortality being admitted, on arguments drawn from the constitution of human nature, and on the authority of the Christian revelation, human nature assumes a degree of dignity which claims the highest respect, and human life becomes a scene of action infinitely important. If an ancient painter, who had with indefatigable attention and perseverance wrought up the productions of his pencil to the greatest perfection in his power, thought it a sufficient apology for his assiduity to say—" I paint for eternity;" how much more justly may
every

every believer in a future state vindicate the most exact attention to his moral conduct, by saying—" I live for eternity!"

Life being, in every point of view, of such great value and importance, wisdom and duty require that it be entered upon with deliberation and foresight. As soon as the powers of the mind are so far matured as to be capable of forming a judgment concerning the ends of living and the means of attaining them, every young person ought to inform himself upon these subjects with all the accuracy in his power, and to lay down to himself some clear and certain principles and rules of conduct. Before a prudent man sets out upon a journey, he first satisfies himself that he has good reasons for undertaking it, and then takes care to obtain all requisite information concerning the road he is to travel, and to make all necessary provision for his safe and comfortable passage. When any one purposes to build a house, before he executes his design, fign, he determines accurately the purpofes of utility, convenience, or ornament, for which it is to be erected, forms a plan as fuitable as poffible to his views, eftimates the coft, and provides the neceffary materials. If in any fingle undertaking fuch precaution be neceffary, how much more in executing the great defign of paffing a refpectable, ufeful, and happy life! Can it be fuppofed, that whilft other arts are only to be acquired by affiduous attention and exercife, no thought or pains are requifite in learning and practifing the moft important of all arts, that of happinefs? The fact is, as the hiftory of mankind fufficiently proves, that the attaining of true and permanent felicity is as difficult as it is defirable.

Young perfons in the purfuit of happinefs are liable to many hindrances and feductions, of which they feldom are duly apprifed, which renders it neceffary that they exercife the utmoft circumfpection and vigilance. Not having had fufficient

ficient experience of the fallibility of their own judgment to lead them to diftruft themfelves, they are prone to form their opinions with precipitation, and to adhere to them with confidence. The ardour of fpirit which fo forcibly impels them to action, renders it irkfome to them to examine things with that patient attention which is requifite to fecure them from error. Prefuming, for want of a more perfect acquaintance with the objects around them, that every thing is what it feems, they are in continual danger of being impofed upon by falfe appearances. They flatter themfelves, that wherever they meet with prefent enjoyment they muft find real happinefs; and they are too eager after the prize which is prefented before them to be fcrupuloufly exact in eftimating its true value. In making this precipitate and hazardous choice, they are encouraged by numerous examples of young men, whofe engaging manners render even their follies and
vices

vices enchanting; and thefe external enticements not unfrequently receive powerful aid from the peculiar caſt of the natural difpofition. On the one hand, a gentle yielding temper fometimes renders falfe fhame, a fear of incurring ridicule, or a defire of obliging, more dangerous fnares than even the folicitations of appetite and paffion. On the other hand, a young man of a bold and daring temper will often be more powerfully feduced into exceffes, by the foolifh ambition of being admired and applauded by his companions as a youth of fpirit, than by any defire of criminal indulgence. Againſt thefe fnares nothing can be an effectual guard but a determined refolution, at all events, ſtrictly to adhere to a plan of life, deliberately formed upon the principles of reafon and religion.

Why is it that we fee fo many young men addicting themfelves to the groffeft debauchery, but becaufe they have never purfued thofe reflections on the nature and foundation of human happiness which would have convinced them of the dangerous and ruinous consequences of licentious gratifications? Because their minds have been never elevated by the contemplation of truth and wisdom above the low pleasures of sense and appetite. Whence does it so frequently happen that young persons, whose early habits and connexions preserve them from all infamous irregularities, nevertheless indulge a frivolous and dissipated turn of mind, which wholly incapacitates them for finding enjoyment in the pursuit of knowledge, the cultivation of taste, or the exercise of some laudable and useful occupation—pass the most precious years of their lives in an uninterrupted succession of amusements, public or private, in which, though the eye or the ear may meet with a transient gratification, the heart can find no solid delight; and at last, when the dream of folly is over, and life calls for its serious cares and duties,

are

are wholly unqualified to fupport the character, and indifpofed to difcharge the offices, of the parent, the friend, the citizen, and the man? The true reafon is, that, at their entrance upon the world, they have never interrupted their gay purfuits, and retired from the crowd, to afk themfelves whence they came, for what end they were created, and what is the great bufinefs of life. To what caufe, moreover, is it to be afcribed, that other young men, who are of a lefs volatile temper, or whofe fituation in life has led them to make profit rather than pleafure the principal object of their attention, fometimes prematurely difcover, not only the prudence, but even the avarice of age, and become ready fcholars and expert practitioners in all the fordid arts of gain? It is unqueftionably owing to a culpable neglect, either in themfelves or their parents, of that moral inftruction which would have furnifhed them with fteady principles of honefty and integrity, and inspired them with liberal and generous sentiments.

In all these cases, and in every other in which young men fail of attaining that true merit which alone can render them respectable and happy, the failure is to be imputed to the want of fixed principles, and a settled plan of conduct. In order to escape the vices and follies of youth, and obtain the possession of that happiness which the nature and condition of man give him a right to expect, it is above all things necessary that young persons look before them, and mark with an attentive eye the track which they ought to pursue. They should neither be contented to adopt whatever plan of living accident may cast in their way, nor suffer their characters to be moulded after the opinions or humours of others; but should be careful to furnish themselves, by diligent inquiry and reflection, with practical principles of religion and maxims of prudence.

To enable a young man to form a plan of conduct to which he may safely adhere through the whole courfe of life, two things are requifite: Firft, that he acquire a clear idea of the nature, and eftablifh a full conviction of the obligations, of morality and religion; fecondly, that he ftudy his own particular capacity, temper, relations, and condition in life. The former is neceffary, as the bafis of every genuine virtue; the latter, as the means of defending him againft feduction, and giving confiftency and ftability to his character.

Let his firft concern, then, be to know what is good, and why it is fo. Let him confult his own underftanding and feelings, and obferve the events which happen in the world, to learn what courfe of conduct is in the nature of things wife, proper, and right, in a human being. Let him ftudy his own powers and inclinations, in order to judge in what manner his time and faculties may be moſt advantageouſly employed. Let him ſearch into the hidden receſſes of his own heart, to explore every latent propenſity towards any kind of criminal indulgence. Let him ſcrutiniſe, with the utmoſt attention, the particular caſt of natural temper by which he is diſtinguiſhed. Let him carefully obſerve what habits have already gained the firmeſt hold upon his mind; that, diſcovering the feeble ſide of his virtue, he may learn towards what points he ought principally to direct his vigilance and circumſpection. Let him, moreover, attend to the ſeveral relations in which he ſtands to ſociety, and ſurvey the advantages and opportunities which his natural or acquired talents, his wealth or influence, afford him of doing good; that he may acquire a proper ſenſe of the obligations which theſe circumſtances lay him under to active exertions in the ſervice of mankind.

In this manner let every young perſon, as ſoon as he arrives at years of diſcretion, make his entrance into the world—with deliberate meditations on the ſcene which lies before him; with ſerious reflections on the importance of human life; with rational principles of morals and religion; with a prudent and well-digeſted plan of life; and with determined reſolution to adhere to that path which his reaſon and judgment have led him to chooſe, as the path of ſafety and happineſs. He will then purſue his journey through life in a ſteady courſe of manly virtue, unſeduced by the allurements which may aſſault him on the right-hand and on the left. In the midſt of the applauſes of the wiſe and good among his fellow-creatures, ſurrounded with the fruits of his early virtues, and triumphing in the conſciouſneſs of having made a wiſe and happy choice, he will go on his way rejoicing,

ing, and will experience the path of the juſt to be " as the ſhining light which ſhineth more and more unto the perfect day."

The Nature, Caufes, and Folly, of Self-deception.

PROVERBS xvi. 3.

All the ways of a man are clean in his own eyes, but the Lord weigheth the fpirits.

PROVERBIAL maxims are commonly to be underftood with certain limitations. The maxim; that all the ways of a man are clean, or right, in his own eyes, though univerfal in the expreffion, evidently admits of many exceptions, both with refpect to the perfons by whom the judgment in queftion is formed, and with refpect to the judgment itfelf. Solomon neither meant to affert that no man whatever

ever is sufficiently enlightened, or sufficiently honest, to confess, at least to his own heart, the faults of his character; nor that those who are the most partial to themselves, never perceive any thing reprehensible in their conduct, or see reason to charge themselves with criminality or imprudence. His design, undoubtedly, is only to affirm, in general, that there are few people in the world who are not disposed to err, on the side of candour, in judging of themselves; and that it is no unusual thing for men to attend only to the fair side of their characters, to applaud themselves for actions which are in reality deserving of censure, and to find a thousand ways of extenuating faults which they cannot but perceive. Solomon speaks of this kind of self-deception as universal, because his knowledge of mankind and of his own heart had taught him that it was exceedingly common.

Wherein consists the exact nature of this moral disease? And to what causes *of Self-deception.*

is it chiefly to be ascribed? If we wish, my brethren, to be aware of our own danger, and to escape it, we must endeavour to solve these questions. Let us begin with the first, and attempt to ascertain the precise nature of the charge which Solomon brings against mankind, when he says—"All the ways of man are clean in his own eyes."

The fault, in general terms, is the forming too advantageous an opinion of ourselves and our actions. It is that kind of delusion which consists in presuming, upon the slightest grounds, that we are free from guilt, or possessed of superior wisdom and merit. No terms could more accurately express the hasty and superficial view upon which these partial judgments are commonly formed than those of the text—" The ways of a man are pure in his own eyes:" they appear upon the first superficial glance to be right, and he does not give himself the trouble to

look

look more accurately into the matter, for he is willing to be deceived.

If, indeed, after ſeriouſly examining his views, his actions, and the motives by which he is governed, any one finds that they are, in general, conformable to the rules which conſcience preſcribes, and to the laws which religion enjoins, nothing can be more reaſonable than that he ſhould enjoy the ſatisfaction of virtuous ſelf-approbation. Such ſatisfaction has a real foundation: it is the firſt fruit and the firſt recompence of virtue. But if any one, haſtily taking appearances for realities, aſcribes to himſelf virtues which he does not poſſeſs, it is evident that his ſelf-applauſe is deluſive, and that the tranquillity which it produces is nothing better than a falſe ſecurity. He is like a man in a dropſy, who miſtakes for ſigns of eſtabliſhed health the firſt ſymptoms of a malady which will ſoon bring him to the grave. He imagines himſelf poſſeſſed of the

the fubftance, where there is, in truth, nothing but the fhadow: if he difcovers in himfelf any qualities really good, he magnifies them beyond their worth: in fhort, through the fafcinating influence of felf-love, he is incapable of feeing his own character in its true light.

I am aware that the natural operation of felf-love to produce felf-deceit is often interrupted by the interference of other paffions. Whilft we are bufily occupied in the purfuit of external objects, we have little leifure even for thofe reflections which are the food of conceit: but, in the midft of all our moft eager purfuits, the artful flatterer, Self-love, finds intervals of repofe, in which fhe holds up her deceitful mirror before our eyes, and tempts us to think of ourfelves more highly than we ought to think. Subtle and ingenious in her devices, the impoftor affumes a thoufand forms, and practifes a thoufand arts, to extenuate or conceal our faults, or to fpread a falfe luftre over our virtues.

virtues. Even those who imagine themselves most superior to her power often find themselves mistaken. The philosopher who fancies that he has discovered all her artifices, the orator who dedescribes them, the casuist who exposes them, and even the saint who boasts that he is above their reach, all pay homage, without perceiving it, to this divinity. And what most of all shews the force and extent of her empire is, that neither age nor experience are a sufficient defence against her power. Self-love is an infirmity which never forsakes us as long as we live. That we may, however, be guarded as much as possible against the inconveniences arising from this passion, let us proceed to consider more distinctly the *symptoms* by which it is discovered. The principal of these are *pride*, *vanity*, *ambition*, and *presumption*.

What is pride, but one of the most disgusting fruits of self-love, which is continually cherished in its growth by self-admiration?

admiration? To be blind to our faults; always to view our virtues through a medium which either magnifies or multiplies them; by an unfair comparifon, to pretend to a fuperiority of merit which tarnifhes or eclipfes the luftre of another's excellencies; to forget ourfelves fo far as even to lift a haughty and confident eye towards heaven, and fay—" God, I thank thee I am not as other men;" is it poffible that we fhould contemplate fuch a character without difguft even in ourfeves, were it not that "all the ways of a man are right in his own eyes?"

What, again, is *vanity*, but an oftentatious difplay of the good qualities and accomplifhments of which we fuppofe ourfelves poffeffed? Puffed up with conceit, and happy in the admiration of himfelf, the vain man is continually endeavouring to attract the notice of others. He makes ufe of every artifice to difplay to the greateft advantage that merit which, he has no doubt, will bear to be expofed in the full face of day. Sometimes he directly affails your judgment, and demands your applaufe, by affuming an haughty and oftentatious air, and confidently making the moft extravagant pretenfions. At another time he veils his vanity under the colouring of a feigned humility, and invites, whilft he feems to avoid, admiration. Whence is all this, but becaufe his " ways are right in his own eyes?"

Who can doubt that *ambition*, or an infatiable thirft after diftinction and power, proceeds from the fame fource? The man who fancies himfelf capable of every thing, will naturally think himfelf worthy of every thing. We are often aftonifhed to fee men, who have little merit and fmall talents, boldly afpiring to places of the firft diftinction and importance, and engaging in difficult enterprifes with the fulleft affurance of fuccefs. Our furprife would ceafe, if we could view their talents and merit with the fame eyes with which they

they are seen by themselves. They know none better qualified than they for the office or undertaking in question; and therefore think it beneath them to resign their pretensions in favour of any man living.

The last characteristic symptom of the moral malady I am describing is *presumption*. If excessive self-love leads a man, through *pride*, to esteem himself too highly, through *vanity* to be too eager after applause, and through *ambition* to aspire at things too high for him, it is the same passion which makes him presume too much upon his own strength, repose with too much security upon his own wisdom, and with too much confidence promise himself success in whatever he undertakes. No expectation is too chimerical for him to entertain: no enterprise too hazardous for him to attempt. Are sagacity and industry necessary to his success, he is happy in being conscious that he possesses them. Are resolution and

and perseverance requisite, in these qualities he is not deficient. Are difficulties to be encountered, and obstacles to be removed, he trusts he has within himself sufficient resources for every exigency.

Such are the principal features of the character which Solomon exhibits in the text, that of one who is so far imposed upon by the delusions of self-love as to become a dupe to pride, ambiton, vanity, and presumption.

Numerous are the causes which concur to produce that confusion of ideas, and those false judgments, which render " all the ways of a man right in his own eyes."

At the head of these we ought undoubtedly to place bad education and early prejudices. Are the dispositions, let it be honestly confessed, with which children are first inspired, ordinarily those of humility, modesty, and a prudent distrust of themselves? Are they taught to value themselves only in proportion as they find

of Self-deception. 405

find themselves, upon mature examinaton, possessed of real merit? Are they instructed never to prefer shewy accomplishments to solid worth; and, above all things, to detest an artificial character, and the affectation of amiable dispositions and good qualities to which they are in reality strangers? In a word, are children taught to *be* virtuous, or to *appear* so; to *merit* distinction, or to *seek for* it? Alas! who does not see, that in the education of children more labour is commonly bestowed upon the external appearance than upon the heart! Whatever is adapted to please, to amuse, and to attract admiration, they are industriously instructed to value and to acquire; and the pains which are taken for this purpose are seldom lost. Upon this frivolous plan their taste is too commonly formed. The consequence is, that exteriors attract their principal attention, they judge of themselves, as of others, from what *appears*, without giving themselves the trouble to inquire what *is*. Provided that their ways *seem* right, it is enough; they take no pains to examine whether they *are* so in reality.

The evil, however, would not be without remedy, if, to the defects of education, we did not add a perverse and obstinate neglect of self-infpection. If, as reason advances towards maturity, young persons would employ themselves in attentively considering the real nature of those qualities upon which they are inclined to value themselves, and carefully reviewing those actions which they have suffered to pass without censure, there can be no doubt that the false lustre which a bad education has spread over their characters would soon be dissipated, and that they would learn to judge of themselves according to nature and truth. But where shall we find the persons who undertake this useful exercise, who apply themselves to this important study? Shall we seek for them among those who are afraid of nothing so much as finding themselves alone;

alone; among thofe who, from morning to evening, and from day to day, are borne away in the vortex of diffipation; or among thofe who are abforbed in cares which leave them no intervals of relaxation? Shall we be affured of finding them even among thofe who profefs to devote one day in feven to the great purpofe of moral and religious improvement? Are not the wifeft and beft among us too apt to neglect the opportunities which thefe intervals afford us for communing with our own hearts, or, however, to content ourfelves with general and fuperficial inquiries, without difturbing our confciences upon thofe points where we have a fecret fufpicion that all is not perfectly right. Even thefe flight reviews are taken under the powerful influence of felf-love: we wifh to think well of ourfelves, we are content to be impofed upon. If our ways *feem right*, without farther inquiry we applaud ourfelves, and contentedly remain juft as we were.

Not that it never happens that we examine ourselves with greater care and diligence. There are seasons of calamity or affliction in which we are disposed to apply ourselves with more than ordinary seriousness to this duty. There are moments in which we feel ourselves dissatisfied with the world, and the things which are in the world, and are inclined to listen to the voice of reason and religion. At such a moment conscience reclaims its rights; speaks, censures, reproaches, and will be heard. But, alas! even in this situation, so favourable to the necessary inquiry, self-love is not without expedients to carry on its deceptions. If we must examine ourselves, it persuades us to do it indirectly by comparison with others, rather than by an immediate appeal to the Eternal Law of Truth. Sometimes we apologise to ourselves for whatever might seem amiss in our conduct by pleading the irresistible force of example, and are satisfied with reflecting that we have

have only followed the fashion of the times, and done what those, who are commonly esteemed good people, are accustomed to do. Sometimes we justify ourselves upon opposite ground: like the Pharisee in the parable, bless God that we are not chargeable with the faults of this or the other man, and rejoice that we have more charity than one neighbour, or more piety than another. Thus we conclude our ways to be right, either because they agree with the ways of the world, or because they are not in some respects so irregular as those of many around us. What principle but self-love could satisfy itself with such feeble supports, or enable man to pronounce, upon such doubtful proofs, that their ways are right?

I must not omit to mention another cause of that kind of self-deception which is characterised in the text, namely, *flattery*. Though this is a snare to which the great are peculiarly exposed, every one

one in his sphere, according to the rank he holds, the authority with which he is invested, the riches he possesses, the talents by which he is distinguished, or the personal graces with which he is adorned, has more or less to apprehend from the pestilential influence of adulation. Where is the man so perfectly free from pride and vanity as not to be elated, beyond the bounds of moderation, by meeting with attention and applause beyond his merits? Nothing is more apt to pervert the judgment and corrupt the heart than the delusions which come from this quarter. Whilst every voice either openly declares or secretly whispers our praise, it will scarcely be in the power of conscience to gain a hearing when it contradicts the report. We shall be rather inclined to believe all the world when it speaks well of us, than to pay attention to the whispers of our own hearts to the contrary.

Lastly, there is no artifice by means of which men more frequently impose upon

of Self-deception.

upon themselves, than by substituting a supposed rectitude of intention in the room of rectitude of conduct. It is true, we generally reserve this apology to the last, because it implies a mortifying confession that we have *acted* wrong. But when other excuses fail, every one knows that this is our last and main resource. "We have acted wrong, it is true, but not designedly: had we seen and known as much before we committed the fault as we have done since, we should have acted very differently." If we have gone astray, it has been through an error in judgment, or through the sudden impulse of passion; we have, notwithstanding, meant well, and it is principally by the intention that the merit or demerit of actions is determined. If our *ways* themselves have not been clean, we persuade ourselves that our *principles*, and *intentions* at least, are pure, that our *hearts* are right in the sight of God. Whereas nothing is more certain, that every tree is known

known by its fruit, and that " he only who doth righteousness is righteous."

In this manner it is, my brethren, that we impose upon ourselves, and imagine ourselves to be other beings than we are. Thus do bad education, superficial self-inspection, unfair comparisons, flattery, and a reliance on mere intentions, all concur to confirm the delusion which self-love is ever ready to encourage.

But, alas! unfortunate is the delusion, and fatal the security; for though " all the ways of a man are clean in his own eyes, the Lord weigheth the spirits."

There is a Supreme Judge, who holds in his hand an unerring balance, in which he weighs with perfect exactness the actions, and even the thoughts and purposes, of men, that he may appreciate their true merit, and regulate their eternal destiny, according to the result of the important trial. The balance in which he weighs the characters of men is the Eternal Law of Righteousness. Himself
perfectly

perfectly juft, wife, and good, it is impoffible that he fhould not conduct this judgment with ftrict impartiality, or that he fhould fail to render to every man according to his works. In eftimating our own characters, we are feldom at the pains to weigh them with an accurate beam, with a fteady hand, and an impartial eye. We are more commonly contented to judge of them by a hafty and fuperficial glance, in which the eye is chiefly attracted by fplendid appearances. But when God weighs our characters he brings every work into judgment with every fecret thing, whether it be good or whether it be evil. Nothing efcapes his notice; nothing comes before him under falfe colours. Before his eye appearances vanifh; realities remain entire. He judges by that which *is*, not by that which only *seems*: the Lord looketh at the heart, the Lord weigheth the fpirits. He examines motives and intentions as well as actions. In his faithful balance,

affected

affected virtue, and hypocritical devotion, are lighter than vanity. What passes upon the world for genuine zeal is in many cases found to be nothing better than a malignant spirit of bigotry and persecution: apparent prudence and frugality is discovered to be real avarice: in short, every counterfeited semblance of virtue is detected; and nothing passes any longer for more than it is worth.

And for what purpose is this strict scrutiny? Is it not, that whatever is found deficient may be rejected, and that whatever will stand the trial may be lodged in the treasury of heaven? To drop the figure—Our Great Creator has placed us in this world as candidates for eternal felicity: to qualify us for it, he has required us to form the genuine habits of virtue and piety. If according to the measure of our knowledge and ability we do this, he will pronounce us worthy of everlasting life, and receive us into that glorious state of perfection and happiness which

which he has provided for good men: but, if our profession of religion be infincere, and our practice of virtue nothing better than mere pretence, he will declare us unfit for the fociety of upright men made perfect, and will confign us to that ftate of punifhment which his wifdom fhall fee neceffary to provide for the correction and final deftruction of vice.

Such is the doctrine of the holy fcriptures; fuch are the ideas which reafon inftructs us to entertain concerning the moral government of God.

Since, then, it is a certain truth, that whatever a man foweth that fhall he alfo reap—how unreafonable, how foolifh is it for men to impofe upon themfelves by vainly imagining that they are in the path of life, when the truth is, that they are in the way which leadeth to deftruction! If God cannot be deceived, and will not be mocked, why fhould men endeavour to deceive themfelves? Why fhould they fpeak peace to themfelves, when in reality

there

there is no peace? And we have the word of Eternal Truth to affure us, that "there *is* no peace to the wicked."

Be it, then, my brethren, your daily care to confider your ways, as under the eye of that Great Being who fees all your actions, who hears all your words, who reads all your thoughts. Confider your paft ways, to difcover and correct your errors: confider your future ways, that they may be clean, not only in your own eyes, but in the eyes of him who weigheth the fpirits; and may the Eternal Spirit teach you the true knowledge of yourfelves, and lead you in the way to life everlafting! 'Amen.

Contentment and Generosity exemplified in the Conduct of Esau.

GENESIS xxxiii. 9.

And Esau said, I have enough, my brother; keep that thou hast unto thyself.

THESE words are part of a pleasing and instructive story, in which we have a lively picture of the strong emotions of affection and joy with which those who have been long at variance meet each other upon an unexpected reconciliation.

Jacob had by an artful contrivance obtained that blessing from his father for himself which had been intended for his elder

elder brother. This so far provoked Esau's resentment, that he determined to avenge himself upon Jacob, after their father's death, by taking away his life. " He said in his heart, The days of mourning for my father are at hand: then will I slay my brother Jacob." As soon as Jacob had information of his brother's design, he thought it necessary to quit his father's house, and went to reside at a considerable distance with his uncle Laban. After an interval of many years, during which he had become the head of a numerous family, and acquired large possessions, he formed the purpose of attempting a reconciliation with his brother Esau. He could not enjoy perfect satisfaction in the midst of his abundance, whilst he recollected the alienation which subsisted between himself and one whom nature had united to him by the most tender ties; and he entertained an hope that long absence and a change of circumstances might have cooled the resentment of his brother, and prepared him for a reconciliation. His sense of duty instructed him, that having himself caused the separation, the first step towards a reunion ought to be on his part; and his remaining affection for his brother rendered this no difficult task. Accordingly he sent messengers to Esau to inquire after his welfare, and propose an interview. On their return, however, when they told him that Esau was coming to meet him with four hundred men, he began to apprehend that his brother still meditated revenge, and prepared to appease his anger by valuable presents. These fears being removed by a vision, Jacob went out to meet his brother, and, as he approached, paid him the utmost respect, bowing, according to the custom of the times, to the ground. Esau, overcome by this submissive behaviour, and by the pleasure of seeing a brother after so many years absence, ran to meet him, and fell on his neck and kissed him. Resentment could now find no place in his breast, for it was wholly possessed by the milder passions of love and joy. Jacob, too, was transported with pleasure to receive such expressions of tender affection from one from whom he had expected nothing less than hostile violence, and to find that union of hearts which nature had established between them, but which his own treachery had destroyed, so happily and unexpectedly restored. Both felt emotions which nothing but tears could express: both wept. After their first transports were over, Jacob informed Esau that the cattle which he had brought with him were intended as a present; which, after much importunity, Esau accepted. Then, taking an affectionate leave of each other, they pursued their respective journeys.

This interesting portion of scripture-history, considered at large, might suggest to our thoughts many useful reflections: but it is my design, in this discourse, to confine your attention to the reply which

Esau

Esau made to Jacob when he offered him a part of his subſtance. Eſau ſaid—" I have enough, my brother: keep that thou haſt unto thyſelf." This reply was evidently dictated by a *contented* and a *generous* ſpirit.

Although Eſau was not the perſon whom God thought proper to chooſe as the founder of the Jewiſh nation, it doth not appear from any circumſtance in his hiſtory that he was a bad man. It is manifeſt from the narrative that he had baniſhed from his breaſt the ſpirit of revenge which he once indulged, and was capable of practiſing that nobleſt virtue, the forgiveneſs of injuries. No objection to the goodneſs of his character ariſes from the words of the prophet Malachi, ch. i. 2, 3, " Jacob have I loved, and I hated Eſau," quoted by the apoſtle Paul in his epiſtle to the Romans; becauſe both the prophet and the apoſtle are ſpeaking concerning them as they were the heads of their reſpective poſterity, and only aſſert, in a mode of expreffion ufual both in the Old Teftament and the New, that God had diftinguifhed Jacob and his defcendants by privileges and bleffings which Efau and his offspring never enjoyed. But, whatever was Efau's general character, it is evident, that in the affair we have been confidering, and particularly in the declaration of the text, he difcovered amiable and worthy difpofitions. Though he had been deprived of a privilege which he highly valued, and which he had been taught to confider as his natural right, Providence had fo far confirmed his father's bleffing by making his dwelling the fatnefs of the earth, that he faw fufficient reafon to be contented and happy in the ftation allotted him, and could fay, even to that brother whom he once fo greatly envied, *I have enough.*

Whither, my brethren, fhall we go to find the man, who, with the full and unwavering affent of his mind, can adopt this language? Miftake not my meaning
fo

so far as to suppose that I ask where the man is to be found who would refuse a larger portion of happiness than he at present enjoys, if it were the will of Heaven to grant it. He who could do this, would be no longer a rational being; for he would have lost the first principle of action, the love of happiness. My inquiry is after the happy man, who is easy in the situation which his Maker has assigned him, and satisfied with the blessings which he is permitted to enjoy.

Visit the mansions of the great, and the palaces of the mighty: observe the splendour and magnificence of their appearance, the extent of their possessions, the variety of their amusements, the deference with which they are every where received, and the homage which they are able to command from their inferiors and dependants. " What can these men want which it is in the power of human nature to enjoy? If contentment is any where to be found on earth, it must surely be amongst those whom fortune hath thus exalted." Such, perhaps, would be the first reflection of a superficial observer. But continue amongst them till you cease to be dazzled by the glare of external pomp; take notice of the envy and jealousy which are continually rising between rival candidates for posts of honour and profit; observe how frequently it happens, that in the midst of affluence and grandeur, they lose the enjoyment of their present possessions through an impatient desire of some object yet unobtained—an object, perhaps, of no greater value, in comparison with the treasures they already possess, than the vineyard of Naboth, which Ahab would neither eat nor sleep till he obtained, in comparison of the kingdom of Israel—follow them into the scenes of private life, and there remark how little satisfaction they appear to find in their enjoyments, and how frequently disappointment and satiety embitter their cup of pleasure, and care and

fretfulness

fretfulness banish sleep from their pillows:—what will be the consequence of your scrutiny? Perhaps you will despair of finding a man among them who is so perfectly contented with his present possessions as to be able to say—" I have enough :" at least you will conclude that real contentment is as seldom found in the palaces of the great as in the cottages of the poor.

Shall we then seek the man who can adopt the words of Esau in the text, among the busy tribe of those, who, in order to increase their substance, rise early, sit up late, and eat the bread of carefulness? If we are to judge from the restless spirit with which many persons belonging to this class pursue their schemes of gain, even to the neglect of every other concern; from the dishonourable and unlawful means which they often make use of to get riches; and from the impatience with which their hopes settle upon some distant good, as that which will prove the consummation of their wishes and the completion of their happiness; we must conclude, that in the middle stations of life there are comparatively few who are duly sensible of the advantages of their situation, and can heartily join in the wise prayer of Agur—" Give me neither poverty nor riches: feed me with food convenient for me."

If in the higher classes of society we meet with such multitudes unsatisfied with their present possessions, uneasy in their present condition, and impatient in the pursuit of some absent good, what success can we expect to meet with by continuing our search after contentment among the lower ranks of mankind! When it is considered to how much labour, hardship, and fatigue, they are subject, with what difficulty and anxiety many among them acquire even necessary supports, and how few of the amusements and luxuries of life, with which others abound, lie within their reach;

little

little room will be left to wonder that so few persons among this class of mankind are so far contented and satisfied with their lot as to be able to say—" I have enough."

Upon a distinct survey of the several ranks of society, we are then necessarily led to this conclusion, that no situation, however easy—none of the gifts of fortune, however liberally bestowed—nor any external circumstances whatever, are sufficient of themselves to produce contentment.

If, therefore, we would discover the man who esteems the portion of good which Heaven hath allotted him *enough*, and can be happy without a prospect of more, we must make use of some other more certain test than men's situation and circumstances in life. Find the man who has learned that happiness arises from a well-ordered and self-approving mind alone—who, from a full conviction of this truth, has by a steady course of virtuous

tuous conduct established the harmony of his affections, and secured the testimony of a good conscience—who firmly believes that all events are under the direction of perfect wisdom and goodness, and will, in their remote connexions and final issues, promote the happiness of the righteous—who enjoys the consolatory persuasion that the wise and good Governor of the world is his Father and Friend—steadily and cheerfully relies on his protection and blessing, and entertains a joyful hope that he will conduct him by the safest and best way to final happiness: this is the man—even if you find him dwelling in a cottage, clad in the meanest attire, sitting down to a coarse and scanty meal, or retiring to rest upon a bed of straw—who enjoys his humble pittance with a relish which a prince might envy; who thanks God that he wants no good thing; and, if you inquire into the state of his mind in his humble condition, will tell you, with hearty content

tent and honest simplicity, that *he has enough*.

Ye sons of ambition, avarice, and luxury, who ransack all the stores of grandeur, wealth, and pleasure, in search of happiness, cease your vain pursuits; turn your eyes towards this good man; mark well his character and his state, and learn to be happy.

To be content with such things as we have is the way to avoid a thousand restless thoughts and uneasy apprehensions. This temper, without preventing us from exercising a proper degree of attention and industry in the management of our affairs, will preserve us in a state of tranquillity highly favourable to the enjoyment of life. It will effectually secure us from the violent agitations and grievous disappointments to which a discontented and covetous disposition is continually subject: and how painful these frequently are the following story may assist us in conceiving.

A young

A young man, who was bleffed with health, genius, and a competent fhare of the gifts of fortune, enjoyed them for feveral years without any material interruption, and had every reafon to expect the continuance of his tranquillity to the end of his days: when, happening one day to walk among the tombs of his anceftors, he obferved upon one of them the following infcription almoft erafed by time—" In this tomb is a greater treafure than ever Crœfus poffeffed." Immediately inflamed with the luft of avarice, he caufed the fepulchre to be opened; when, entering with rapturous expectation of finding immenfe treafures, he was ftruck fpeechlefs with difappointment to behold nothing but a heap of bones, duft, and putrefaction, with this infcription over it—" Here would have remained *Eternal Repofe,* a treafure which Crœfus never poffeffed; but thou haft driven it from hence, excited by an infatiable love of gold to difturb the facred remains

remains of thy anceftors. Go hence, and learn wifdom."

Such mortification muft all thofe meet with who, not contented with what they at prefent enjoy, expect to be happy in fome diftant good: and whilft the difcontented man is perpetually expofed to the vexations of difappointment, he is liable to have his peace difturbed by the painful emotions of envy. In the midft of plenty, he will be incapable of relifhing his own ftores, becaufe his neighbour poffeffes more. Whereas the contented man taftes all the delights which naturally belong to his condition, and even makes the poffeffions of others his own, whilft every agreeable object which furrounds him, whoever be the poffeffor, ferves to convey pleafure to his heart. Thus fecure from the unquiet perceptions of difcontent and envy, his mind is calm and unruffled; his fpirits flow in a fteady current of innocent cheerfulnefs, which diffufes health and vigour through his frame,

and

and spreads serenity and gladness over his countenance.

Nor are the advantages of a contented temper confined to a man's self. He who thinks he has already enough of the good things of life, will not be disposed to invade his neighbour's property, to practise the hidden things of dishonesty, or to load his poor dependents with the grievous yoke of oppression.

This temper will, moreover, preserve a man from making use of any mean arts to extort those benefits from others which they are neither bound nor disposed to bestow: on the contrary, he will often generously decline accepting favours when it might betray a selfish temper, or is likely to prove injurious to the donor.

Such was the conduct of Esau in the affair to which the text relates. He was contented and satisfied with his present possessions, and was desirous that his reconciliation with his brother might appear to be what it really was, not the
prudent

prudent expedient of selfishness, but the honest result of natural affection and generosity. Instead, therefore, of eagerly seizing the prize which his brother's goodness had placed in his way, he waved the acceptance of the present with this gentle and courteous apology—" I have enough, my brother: keep that thou hast unto thyself."

After this modest refusal, he could with a better grace receive his brother's kindness, when he urged him a second time, with great importunity, to accept it; for the gift would now appear, not as the purchase of reconciliation, but as the mutual pledge of future love.

This incident instructs us that much delicacy is requisite both in bestowing and in receiving favours. There is a certain kindness in the manner of conferring benefits, without which Charity with one hand stabs a dagger into the heart of those she relieves, whilst she displays her gifts in the other. In like manner there is a graceful

graceful modesty in the manner of receiving favours which conciliates the affections of the donor, and assures him that he has not bestowed his kindness upon an unworthy object. Whereas a forward, disrespectful, or negligent air, is in such a situation a sure indication of pride or insensibility, and affronts the generosity of the benefactor.

But to return to the principal subject of this discourse. Contentment will not only preserve us from meanly abusing or trespassing upon the kindness of others, but will dispose us to be ourselves kind, and bountiful. The man who can say, "I have enough," will not think he has too little, when he has disposed of a small part of his possessions to relieve the wants of others. He will partake of the feast which the God of nature hath provided for him with peculiar pleasure, when he sees the poor and the needy refreshed by the remnants of his board.

A contented mind will prepare us to meet

meet with sudden and unexpected changes in our condition. The same principle which will enable us to be satisfied in one station of life, will inspire us with contentment in another. If a consciousness of upright intentions and a virtuous character enables us to look up to our Maker with humble confidence in his approbation, we may assure ourselves that whatever portion he allots us is intended for our benefit. Enjoying peace in our own minds, and having a good hope towards God, we shall in any situation have enough to ensure our happiness both in this life and that which is to come: we may support ourselves under all the disappointments and calamities of the present state by the prospect of a world in which we shall be able to adopt the language of the text in its utmost extent—where contentment shall be exalted into perfect, uninterrupted, and everlasting enjoyment.

What then remains, but that, by forming just conceptions of the nature of human

man happiness; by living in the determined practice of all those virtues which will furnish us with an inexhaustible fund of pleasing reflections; and by continually exercising a stedfast faith in the providence of God, a patient submission to his will, and a grateful sense of his goodness, and a joyful hope of eternal life, we learn the happy art, in whatever state we are, therewith to be content?

Let your conversation be without covetousness, and be content with such things as ye have; for godliness with contentment is great gain.

END OF THE FIRST VOLUME.

T. Bensley, Printer, Bolt Court, Fleet Street, London.

www.ingramcontent.com/pod-product-compliance
Lightning Source LLC
Chambersburg PA
CBHW022104300426
44117CB00007B/574